Understanding the Roots of Your Mood Swings and
Persistent Feelings of Emptiness

Adele Byrne

borderline personality disorder

A Guide to Living with BPD and
Supporting Loved Ones

ISBN: 979-12-81498-43-3

Contents

INTRODUCTION

As the darkness of an eclipsed sun descends, so too does the complex world of Borderline Personality Disorder (BPD) envelope countless lives in its tangled, enigmatic grasp. Borderline Personality Disorder often finds itself ensnared in the undergrowth of misconception and stigma, an unfortunate companion of many mental health conditions. The lens of media, sharpened to sensationalize, can sometimes cast individuals with BPD as wildly uncontrollable or inherently weak. If you or a loved one carries the burden of a BPD diagnosis, you will find yourselves in a duel, not only with the tumultuous waves of the disorder but also with the stubbornly held prejudices and misconceptions of others.

It's true that BPD can be associated with heightened emotional reactivity, impulsivity, and complex interpersonal relations.

Still, it's critical to remember that these are mere facets of a profound and intricate human experience. The person with BPD is so much more than a collection of stereotyped traits or behaviors. In the pages of this book, we venture beyond the surface of BPD, journeying through its diverse symptoms, exploring its roots, and untangling the complex weave of experiences it brings.

A diagnosis of BPD is not an end, nor is it a dictate to surrender to stereotypes of instability or helplessness. It's a call to arms—a summons to rally courage, engage treatment, and step towards a fulfilling life encompassing a rewarding career, nurturing friendships, and meaningful relationships. This book offers the tools and strategies to harness control over BPD, introducing methods for managing unpredictable emotions and therapies to anchor the emotional storms.

Relating to loved ones can indeed be a delicate dance when you're juggling BPD. The fear of unintentionally hurting those you care about may loom large, given the emotional turbulence associated with BPD. Fear not, though, for this guide will help you communicate your experiences with your family, friends, and partners, fostering understanding and empathy, creating a secure, loving support network.

BPD's impact radiates beyond the individual, reaching out to loved ones who may be equally, if not more, bewildered and distressed. Whether you're a parent, partner, child, or friend of someone with BPD, this book is a hand extended in support. Here, we explore ways to communicate effectively, mitigate conflict, and manage relationships with BPD sufferers.

Protecting your own mental well-being is just as critical when you're in the sphere of influence of someone with BPD. Strategies to disarm manipulation, nurture harmonious relationships, and, if necessary, end relationships with minimal conflict and distress are part of this journey.

Designed with empathy, this book addresses the profound needs of individuals diagnosed with BPD and their loved ones. However, it may not serve those seeking a quick fix or an overnight transformation – the journey to understanding BPD is intricate, necessitating patience and commitment.

For those who doubt, know this: Knowledge is the first step to change. This book is a beacon of understanding, shedding light on the path to managing and overcoming the challenges of BPD.

This resource is not intended to be an academic text, but rather a more accessible and compassionate resource for those who want to learn more about borderline personality disorder. While it is not intended to replace the advice of a qualified mental health professional, it can provide a starting point for understanding this complex condition and the challenges that people with BPD face.

This book stands apart from others in its multifaceted approach to Borderline Personality Disorder. It delves not only into the mechanics of the disorder but also unearths the human experiences beneath the surface. Too often, literature on BPD is clinical and detached, focusing only on symptoms and treatment. This book, however, acknowledges the whole person living with the disorder.

Carrying the diagnosis of BPD is not a life sentence. It's a challenge to surmount, a puzzle to solve. The guidance and tools within these pages are stepping stones towards a fulfilling life for both individuals living with BPD and their loved ones. You are more than your diagnosis; you are a fighter, a survivor, a beacon of resilience and hope.

PART 1: LIVING WITH BORDERLINE PERSONALITY DISORDER

CHAPTER 1: DEFINING BORDERLINE PERSONALITY DISORDER: UNDERSTANDING ITS IMPACT AND IMPLICATIONS

Have you ever wondered why some people struggle with emotional turbulence and impulsivity more than others? Why do some people seem to teeter on the brink of anxiety and psychosis, making it difficult for clinicians to diagnose them? Why do these individuals have low self-esteem and form turbulent relationships?

This section explores the complexities of borderline personality disorder, a fascinating yet debilitating condition that affects approximately 2% of the population.

Borderline Personality Disorder is a complex psychological condition characterized by a pattern of fluctuating mental behaviors that impact a person's ability to manage emotions and impulses effectively. Individuals living with BPD often grapple with emotional turbulence, leading to a pattern of unpredictable and, at times, aggressive behavior. This instability often spills over into their relationships, creating an ongoing cycle of discord in multiple areas of their lives.

The term "borderline" in the context of Borderline Personality Disorder traces back to 1938 and is attributed to the American psychoanalyst Adolph Stern. Stern initially introduced this term to describe a group of patients who demonstrated patterns of behavior that didn't improve with conventional treatment methods. This specific group of patients was seen to straddle the line between neurosis and psychosis, thus giving birth to the term "borderline".

Further, the designation "borderline" was meant to signify patients who were thought to be on the borderline between anxiety and psychosis, due to their tendencies towards anxious behaviors and transient psychotic experiences. These patients appeared to exist on the fringe of established diagnostic categories, making it challenging to diagnose and treat them appropriately. They were neither neurotic nor psychotic, but seemed to exhibit symptoms of both conditions.

With time, the understanding of BPD evolved significantly. It's now recognized as a distinct disorder characterized by mood instability, impulsivity, fear of abandonment, and self-image problems. It became an official personality disorder in 1980, according to the *"Diagnostic and Statistical Manual of Mental Disorders, Third Edition"* (DSM-III). Despite its official recognition, the term "borderline" continues to stir debates regarding its appropriateness and accuracy.

One of the most poignant characteristics of BPD is the constant struggle with self-esteem and self-perception. Those with BPD often harbor recurrent, distressing thoughts about themselves and their interactions with others, leading to a pervading sense of low self-worth. This negative thought pattern can escalate to more harmful behaviors, including self-harm and, in severe instances, suicide.

Borderline personality disorder can have a significant impact on interpersonal relationships. Individuals with BPD often have a deep fear of abandonment and an unstable sense of self. These factors can lead to intense, unstable attachments to others, as well as to **splitting** or **black-and-white thinking**.

Splitting is a cognitive distortion in which people with BPD view others in extremes, as either all good or all bad. This can lead to rapidly changing emotions and behaviors in relationships, as the person with BPD swings between idealizing and devaluing others.

Black-and-white thinking is a related cognitive distortion in which people with BPD see things in absolute terms, with no room for shades of gray. This can make it difficult for people with BPD to tolerate differences of opinion or to see the good in others when they make mistakes.

These cognitive distortions can lead to intense and unstable relationships for people with BPD. They may become overly dependent on others, fearing abandonment, and may react with anger, rage, or despair when they feel rejected. They may also push others away, fearing that they will be hurt if they get too close.

When people with BPD form attachments, they often do so very quickly and intensely. These attachments can be so strong that they may seem obsessive or smothering to others. People with BPD may become overly dependent on their attachments, seeing them as a lifeline and source of validation and emotional stability.

However, these attachments can be fragile and can quickly change. A minor disagreement, perceived slight, or fear of rejection or abandonment can trigger an intense negative reaction. People with BPD may suddenly view the person they once idealized as fundamentally bad, harmful, or rejecting. It can be confusing and distressing not only for the person with BPD but also for those around them who are often left feeling bewildered by these abrupt emotional changes.

It is important to remember that not everyone with BPD will experience all of the symptoms or behaviors listed. The severity of BPD symptoms can vary from person to person, and the expression of the disorder can be influenced by many factors, including other mental health conditions, traumatic experiences, and individual personality traits. We will discuss these factors in more detail in later chapters.

Around 2% of a given population typically meet the criteria for this disorder, with it occurring thrice as much in women, potentially due to societal norms and greater help-seeking behavior. The onset often emerges during adolescence or early adulthood, triggered by significant life changes. As people age, a "burnout" effect may reduce symptom severity. However, individual experiences can greatly vary, influenced by factors such as genetics and environment.

To answer the initial question, although we will explore these concepts in more detail in a later chapter, the etiology of borderline personality disorder is a complex process that involves a variety of factors. It is thought to arise from a combination of factors including environmental, social, neurological, and genetic influences. Significant life events, such as traumatic experiences during childhood, can also serve as triggers.

Frequently, BPD co-exists with other mental health disorders like depression, eating disorders, post-traumatic stress disorder, or bipolar disorder, complicating diagnosis and treatment. Moreover, substance abuse problems are commonly associated with BPD. Despite the significant challenges posed by BPD, it is essential to recognize that the disorder is manageable with appropriate treatment.

Before we move on, let's take a moment to review what we've learned in this chapter:

This chapter has provided an overview of borderline personality disorder, a serious mental health condition that affects how people think, feel, and relate to others. BPD is characterized by intense and unstable emotions, impulsive behavior, and unstable relationships.

Key Points:

- The term "borderline" was first used in the 1930s to describe people who seemed to be on the border between neurosis and psychosis. Today, we know that BPD is a distinct mental health condition that is not caused by either neurosis or psychosis.

- People with BPD often struggle with self-perception and self-esteem. They may have a distorted view of themselves and their worth, which can lead to feelings of intense shame, guilt, and worthlessness. These feelings can be so overwhelming that people with BPD may engage in self-harm or suicide.

- BPD also has a significant impact on interpersonal relationships. People with BPD often have intense, unstable attachments to others. They may idealize people at first, only to devalue them later. They may also have difficulty trusting others and may fear abandonment. These fears can lead to impulsive behavior, such as rage, aggression, or threats of suicide.

- BPD is a relatively rare condition, affecting about 2% of the population. It is more common in women than in men. The onset of BPD usually occurs during adolescence or early adulthood, and symptoms can lessen as people age.

- Borderline personality disorder often co-exists with other mental health conditions, such as depression, eating disorders, post-traumatic stress disorder (PTSD), or bipolar disorder. This can complicate diagnosis and treatment.

Now that we have a basic understanding of borderline personality disorder, we can go into more detail in the next chapter about the most common traits of BPD. This will help us to identify BPD more easily, as sometimes more than one *"conditions"* can coexist in a person, which can mask even the most common traits.

CHAPTER 2: 10 MOST COMMON TRAITS OF PEOPLE WITH BORDERLINE PERSONALITY DISORDER

Do you want to learn more about the specific traits of Borderline Personality Disorder?

As we discussed earlier, people with Borderline Personality Disorder often have co-existing mental health conditions, such as anxiety disorders, eating disorders, and addiction problems. The overlap of symptoms with conditions like bipolar disorder can make it difficult to diagnose BPD.

Let's take a closer look at the key symptoms and characteristics of BPD:

Emotional dysregulation

Emotional dysregulation is a common challenge for people with borderline personality disorder. People with BPD often have difficulty managing their emotions, which can lead to intense, unpredictable, and inappropriate emotional reactions.

People who experience emotional dysregulation may:

- **Feel a high degree of emotional sensitivity**, reacting intensely to situations that many people would find minimally upsetting.

- **Have an exaggerated response to seemingly small triggers**, with their emotions spiking more frequently, rapidly, and intensely than would normally be expected.

- **Swing wildly from intense happiness to severe depression within a matter of hours or even minutes.**

- **Struggle to return to a stable emotional baseline** after experiencing strong emotions.

High emotional intensity

People with this condition often experience emotions with high intensity. Their reactions to events or situations may seem overly intense or exaggerated compared to the actual circumstance. This can make their lives feel like an ongoing "emotional roller coaster."

They may experience rapid, intense mood swings, where states of euphoria can abruptly shift to periods of intense despair within a remarkably short span. The frequency and unpredictability of these emotional shifts can be overwhelming and disruptive to their daily life.

These emotional states are not merely mood swings, but rather profound emotional experiences. Moments of joy can feel exhilarating and all-consuming, while periods of sadness can feel like an inescapable abyss. The emotional world of someone with this condition is one of extreme peaks and valleys, with little time spent on stable, middle ground.

This high emotional intensity can create a sense of instability and unpredictability. It can disrupt their ability to perform regular tasks, maintain relationships, and lead a balanced life. It can also create an internal environment of constant emotional turmoil, causing considerable psychological distress.

Acute Sensitivity to Feedback

Individuals living with this condition often demonstrate a heightened sensitivity to criticism. Even the slightest hint of disapproval can feel like a profound rejection to them. They may perceive criticism, whether intended or not, as a personal attack, which can trigger intense emotional reactions.

It's essential to understand that this reaction isn't an overreaction or an attempt to be dramatic, but rather a fundamental part of their experience. It can feel like they're perpetually walking on a tightrope, where a single misplaced word can lead to an emotional freefall. Navigating the world with this heightened sensitivity can be incredibly challenging and isolating, adding to the complexities of their everyday lives.

Inconsistent Self-Perception and Identity Struggles

Living with this condition often have a wavering sense of self. They may struggle to form a clear understanding of their identities, including personal preferences, beliefs, and long-term goals. This can make decisions related to career paths or relationships particularly challenging, as they may frequently change their minds or feel uncertain about what they truly want.

This inconsistency often extends to their self-image as well. They may oscillate between periods of positive self-regard and periods of intense self-criticism. This rapidly shifting self-image can contribute to feelings of emptiness, confusion, and a lack of direction.

Fearful Avoidance of Abandonment

One of the biggest challenges for people with this condition is an overwhelming fear of being left alone. This fear often stems from traumatic experiences they may have experienced in the past, which we will discuss in Chapter Five.

These individuals crave meaningful relationships and emotional connection. However, they live in constant fear that any sign of conflict or disagreement will drive their loved ones away. This fear can trigger an instinct to avoid rejection, causing them to end relationships or friendships prematurely. They may choose to leave before they feel they could be left.

It is important to understand that these behaviors are driven by fear, not by a desire to hurt others. They are simply trying to protect themselves from what they perceive as inevitable pain.

Extreme Dichotomous Thinking

People with this condition often see the world in extremes, with no middle ground. They may view people, situations, and events as either all good or all bad. This type of thinking is called "dichotomous thinking" or "black-and-white thinking."

For example, someone with dichotomous thinking might see their partner as either perfect or terrible. They might see themselves as either a complete failure or a total success. This type of thinking can be very difficult to live with, as it can lead to a lot of emotional distress.

There are a few reasons why people might develop dichotomous thinking. One reason is that they may have experienced trauma or abuse in their past. This can lead to a belief that the world is a dangerous place and that people cannot be trusted. Another reason for dichotomous thinking is that people may have learned it from their parents or caregivers. If someone grew up in a household where people were always either praised or criticized, they may learn to think in extremes.

Impulsivity

People with this condition often have difficulty controlling their impulses. This can lead to them engaging in potentially harmful or risky behaviors, such as:

- Impulsive spending

- Overeating

- Unsafe sexual practices

- Substance abuse

- Reckless driving

It is important to understand that impulsivity is not always a symptom of this condition. However, when it is, it can be very difficult to control.

There are a few reasons why people with borderline personality disorder might have difficulty controlling their impulses. One reason is that they may have experienced trauma or abuse in their past. This can lead to them feeling out of control and like they need to do something to feel better. Another reason for impulsivity is that people with this condition may have difficulty thinking through the consequences of their actions. They may act without thinking about how their actions will affect themselves or others.

Turbulent Personal Relationships

Those grappling with this condition frequently encounter stormy personal relationships, a consequence of their struggles to regulate emotions and their deeply-rooted fear of abandonment. These individuals might embark on relationships with a sense of intensity, seeing the other party as a potential savior or the perfect partner. However, as soon as they encounter disagreement, conflict, or perceive signs of distance, they may quickly swing to the opposite extreme—seeing the same person as harmful or disappointing.

This emotional pendulum often leads to a cycle of idealization and devaluation, which can be confusing and distressing not only for them but also for their partners, friends, or family. Moreover, due to their sensitivity to rejection and criticism, they may perceive slights or abandonments where none exist, amplifying their emotional response and creating a stormy relationship atmosphere.

Such relational dynamics can leave them feeling insecure and isolated, further exacerbating the cycle of emotional instability. This pattern of tumultuous interpersonal relationships is a central feature of the condition, and it often poses significant challenges to their mental wellbeing, social life, and even occupational functioning.

In the subsequent chapters of the book, we will delve deeper into the intricacies of how this condition influences interpersonal dynamics, explores the coping strategies for those in relationships with affected individuals, and how therapy can help navigate these often volatile relational landscapes.

Self-Harm and Risky Behaviors

People with this condition often engage in self-destructive behaviors as a way to cope with overwhelming emotions. These behaviors can range from sabotaging their academic or professional performance to isolating themselves from others.

The goal of these behaviors is often to temporarily relieve emotional pain. However, the relief is usually short-lived and is followed by feelings of guilt and remorse. This can lead to a cycle of self-destruction, where people engage in harmful behaviors to cope with the guilt, which only leads to more pain and more self-destructive behavior.

Some common forms of self-destructive behavior include eating disorders, substance abuse, self-injury, and risky sexual activity. It is estimated that up to 10% of people with this condition may attempt suicide at some point in their lives.

These self-destructive tendencies are a sign of the severe emotional pain that people with this condition experience. It is important to seek help if you or someone you know is engaging in self-destructive behaviors.

Dissociation

Dissociation is a common coping mechanism that people with borderline personality disorder and other mental health conditions, such as post-traumatic stress disorder (PTSD) and acute stress disorder (ASD), use to deal with overwhelming emotions. It can involve feeling detached from your body, the world around you, or even your own identity.

There are different types of dissociation, including:

- **Depersonalization:** This is a feeling of detachment from your own body or mind. It can feel like you're watching yourself from outside your body, or like you're not really in control of your thoughts or actions. For example, you might feel like your body is moving on its own, or like you're not really feeling the emotions that you're supposed to be feeling.

- **Derealization:** This is a feeling of detachment from the world around you. It can make the world around you seem unreal, dreamlike, or like you're in a haze. For example, you might feel like you're not really in the present moment, or like the world around you is not real.

- **Amnesia:** This is a loss of memory for events or periods of time. The amnesia can be partial or complete, and it can last for a short time or for years. For example, you might forget about a traumatic event, or you might forget about entire weeks or months of your life.

- **Identity confusion:** This is a feeling of uncertainty about who you are. It can make you feel like you don't know yourself, or like you have multiple personalities. For example, you might feel like you're not really the same person you were before a traumatic event, or you might feel like you have different personalities that come out in different situations.

- **Identity alteration:** This is a change in your behavior or personality. It can be caused by a change in your environment, or it can be a way of coping with difficult emotions. For example, you might start acting in a way that is different from your usual self, or you might start to develop new interests or hobbies.

Let us take a quick look at what we have discussed in this chapter:

In this chapter, we discussed the varied and complex symptoms and characteristics of borderline personality disorder. We explored the emotional, cognitive, and behavioral challenges faced by individuals with this condition.

Key Points:

- **Emotional dysregulation:** People with BPD often struggle to control their emotions, leading to unpredictable and intense emotional reactions. They may experience anger, sadness, anxiety, and other emotions intensely and rapidly.

- **High emotional intensity:** BPD sufferers frequently

experience extreme emotional shifts, making their lives feel like an ongoing emotional rollercoaster. They may go from feeling happy to feeling sad, angry, or anxious in a matter of minutes or hours.

- **Acute sensitivity to feedback:** Individuals with BPD have heightened sensitivity to criticism, often perceiving it as a personal attack that can trigger intense emotional reactions. They may take even minor criticisms very personally and may become defensive, angry, or upset.

- **Inconsistent self-perception and identity struggles:** BPD sufferers often have an unstable sense of self, leading to wavering beliefs, preferences, and goals. They may feel like they don't know who they are or what they want out of life.

- **Fearful avoidance of abandonment:** An overwhelming fear of being left alone is common in individuals with BPD. They may feel like they can't survive without the constant support of others. This fear of abandonment can lead to behaviors aimed at keeping people close, such as clinging, possessiveness, or threats of self-harm.

- **Extreme dichotomous thinking:** BPD sufferers often see the world in black and white, without any middle ground. They may view people as either good or bad, friends or enemies, and so on. This black-and-white thinking can lead to significant emotional distress and make it difficult to maintain healthy relationships.

- **Impulsivity:** Difficulty controlling impulses can lead those with BPD to engage in potentially harmful or risky behaviors. This could include substance abuse, reckless driving, unsafe sex, or binge eating.

- **Turbulent personal relationships:** People with BPD often encounter stormy personal relationships due to their emotional instability and fear of abandonment. They may push people away or become clingy and possessive. They may also have difficulty trusting others and may be quick to anger or jealousy.

- **Self-harm and risky behaviors:** To cope with overwhelming emotions, individuals with BPD often engage in self-destructive behaviors, such as self-harm or risky sexual activity. These behaviors may provide temporary relief from emotional pain, but they can lead to long-term problems, such as physical injury, addiction, and depression.

- **Dissociation:** BPD sufferers often experience dissociation as a coping mechanism. Dissociation is a state
  of detachment from reality that can involve feeling
  detached from your body, the world around you, or
  even your own identity. Dissociation can be a way of
  escaping from overwhelming emotions, but it can also
  lead to problems, such as memory loss and difficulty
  concentrating.

Knowing the common symptoms of borderline personality disorder can help you if you believe you or a loved one may be experiencing it. However, there are also a number of subtle signs of BPD that are not as obvious. In the following chapter, we will take a look at some of the more subtle symptoms of BPD and how to identify them.

CHAPTER 3: THE LESS OBVIOUS SIGNS OF BORDERLINE PERSONALITY DISORDER

Do you know someone who seems to be struggling with intense emotions, but they don't seem to be expressing them in a typical way?

If so, they may have a lesser-known form of borderline personality disorder called **"quiet BPD"**.

While the most common symptoms of BPD are easily identifiable, there are also less obvious signs that can be just as important to pay attention to. One lesser-known presentation of BPD is often referred to as **"quiet"** BPD.

Unlike the typical form of BPD, which is characterized by noticeable mood swings, people with quiet BPD primarily internalize their emotional turmoil. This means that they may experience the same intense emotions as someone with BPD, but they may not express them in the same way. Instead, they may withdraw from others, become self-critical, or engage in self-destructive behaviors.

Identifying the presence of "quiet" Borderline Personality Disorder in oneself or others requires a keen observation of certain signs and characteristics. These are as follows:

- **Difficulty in Sustaining Relationships:** Individuals with quiet Borderline Personality Disorder often find it challenging to maintain relationships of any kind. This difficulty is largely due to the individual's unpredictable emotional shifts, which can confuse or scare away the other party in the relationship. Furthermore, the fear of abandonment that is commonly present in individuals with BPD can lead them to prematurely end relationships that they perceive to be struggling, adding to the difficulty of maintaining long-term connections.

- **Decreased Self-Worth:** Those with quiet BPD often struggle with significantly reduced self-esteem. This decrease in self-worth is typically inwardly directed, as the individual often resorts to self-blame and self-degradation. Their self-concept can be so negative that they may commonly use phrases like "I never do anything right" or "Why would anyone want to be around me?" when talking about themselves.

- **Tendencies Towards Self-Harm and Suicidal Ideation:** Individuals with quiet BPD are often at a high risk of self-harm and suicidal ideation. They may express thoughts of self-harm or suicide in an offhand or casual manner, but these comments often mask deeper emotional pain. According to research, about 75% of people with BPD will make at least one suicide attempt in their lifetime.

- **Unhealthy Boundaries:** People with quiet BPD often demonstrate extreme or unhealthy boundaries in their relationships. This might manifest as obsessing over an individual and overly worrying about their opinions, or it could result in complete withdrawal and self-isolation in an effort to create a 'safe' emotional distance from others.

- **Amplified Emotions:** BPD sufferers typically experience emotions more intensely than others. This emotional sensitivity can result in profound feelings of joy, excitement, and love, but it can also lead to being easily overwhelmed by negative emotions such as anxiety, depression, guilt, and anger. The amplification of these emotions can distort the person's reality, turning normal emotions into extreme emotional states.

- **Inability to Concentrate:** A less obvious trait of quiet BPD is the difficulty concentrating. This is often due to the build-up of intense emotions that occupy the mind, resulting in a form of dissociation where the person might appear to be simply spacing out. This could manifest as an emotionless facial expression, monotone speech, or a generally distracted demeanor.

Quiet borderline personality disorder is not an official subtype of BPD, but it is a term used to describe people who meet the diagnostic criteria for BPD but who do not exhibit the typical symptoms of BPD.

Let's recap what we've discussed:

This chapter discussed a less-known form of borderline personality disorder, known as "quiet" BPD. We explored its unique manifestations and characteristics, and contrasted it with more common presentations of BPD.

Key Points:

- **Quiet BPD** is a term that describes people who meet the diagnostic criteria for BPD but who **internalize** their emotional turmoil rather than **externalize** it, which is more typical of BPD.

- People with quiet BPD often find it **challenging to maintain relationships** due to unpredictable emotional shifts and **fear of abandonment**.

- Individuals with quiet BPD **struggle with low self-esteem**, often resorting to **self-blame and self-degradation**.

- There is a **high risk of self-harm and suicidal ideation** among people with quiet BPD.

- People with quiet BPD often **demonstrate extreme or unhealthy boundaries in relationships** and may **struggle with concentration** due to the intensity of their emotions.

- **Despite the differences in presentation, the emotional pain experienced by individuals with quiet BPD is not less than those with typical BPD.**

- **Quiet BPD, although not officially recognized,**

provides a significant lens to understand the complexity and diversity of BPD experiences.

I hope that I have been able to share with you the importance of recognizing the symptoms of borderline personality disorder, both the obvious and the more hidden ones. This knowledge can be helpful in identifying whether you or someone you love may be struggling with this mental health condition. In the next chapter, we will discuss the different types of BPD in more detail.

CHAPTER 4: WHAT ARE THE DIFFERENT TYPES OF BPD?

Have you ever wondered how people with border-line personality disorder experience the disorder differently?

Each person's experience is unique, and their journey with BPD is no different. In the first two chapters, we explored the stark contrast in behavior between those with "quiet" BPD and those with more overt symptoms.

Theodore Millon, a renowned American psychologist, created a framework for understanding the uniqueness of BPD in his 1995 book, *"Disorders of Personality DSM-IV and Beyond."* Millon identified four distinct types of BPD in his framework:

- **Discouraged Borderline:** People with discouraged borderline personality disorder often display behaviors that are similar to those of people with depression, anxiety, or attachment disorders. They may be submissive, humble, and compliant, and they may seem clingy and dependent on others. They may also feel powerless, vulnerable, hopeless, and dejected. This type of BPD is often caused by a fear of abandonment. People with discouraged BPD may have experienced abandonment or rejection in their past, and they may be afraid of being abandoned again. This fear can lead them to become overly dependent on others and to avoid conflict at all costs.

- **Petulant Borderline:** is a subtype of BPD that is characterized by mood swings, passive-aggressive behavior, irritability, low self-esteem, and defiance. People with petulant BPD often feel impatient, resentful, and easily slighted. They may also feel undeserving, disappointed, and angry. They may desperately rely on others one moment and distance themselves the next, out of fear of disappointment or rejection. They may have difficulty tolerating being alone. Their emotions can swing wildly, and their relationship patterns can be unstable. Just like other forms of BPD, petulant BPD can affect how people think and feel about themselves and others. This can lead to problems functioning in everyday life, such as self-image issues, difficulty managing emotions and behavior, and a pattern of unstable relationships.

- **Impulsive borderline:** is a subtype of BPD that is characterized by impulsive behaviors, risky activities, and quick mood swings. People with this disorder often have charismatic and energetic personalities, and they may be drawn to new experiences and thrills. However, this constant need for stimulation can also lead them to make rash decisions without considering the consequences. People with impulsive BPD may also have a fear of abandonment and loss. This fear can cause them to overreact to perceived slights or threats, and it may even lead to suicidal thoughts. Additionally, people with impulsive BPD may have difficulty managing their emotions, which can lead to problems in their relationships and in their overall well-being.

- **Self-destructive borderline:** is another subtype of BPD that is characterized by a persistent feeling of inner turmoil and self-loathing. This can manifest as harmful behaviors directed towards oneself, such as self-harm, self-punishment, reckless driving, neglect of personal health care, and engaging in derogatory sexual acts. These behaviors can put individuals at risk and intensify their feelings of guilt and self-hatred, thereby creating a vicious cycle of self-destruction. Self-destructive BPD is usually diagnosed by a mental health professional based on the presence of certain characteristic signs and symptoms. Treatment typically involves psychotherapy, such as cognitive-behavioral therapy (CBT), dialectical behavior therapy (DBT), mentalization-based treatment (MBT), and transference-focused psychotherapy. These therapies can help individuals develop healthier coping mechanisms, improve their self-perception, and reduce self-destructive behaviors. In some cases, medications may also be prescribed to help manage co-occurring conditions, such as depression or anxiety.

Christine Ann Lawson, Ph.D., a psychologist specializing in BPD, introduced four subtypes of borderline personality disorder in her book *"Understanding the Borderline Mother."* The categories she proposed were based on her observations in clinical settings and her extensive experience working with people with BPD and their families. Here is a brief explanation of the types she proposed:

- **Borderline Queen:** This subtype is characterized by perfectionistic tendencies. Individuals with the Borderline Queen subtype often exhibit an inability to accept criticism and may react aggressively or defensively if they perceive that someone is suggesting they've made a mistake. This can be tied to their need to maintain a flawless image of themselves. They often disassociate from their own negative traits and emotions and might engage in "one-upping" behaviors, attempting to prove their superiority over others, including their therapists and loved ones.

- **Borderline Waif:** The Borderline Waif subtype can be thought of as the "victim" subtype. These individuals generally do not display much aggression or outward hostility. Instead, they often see themselves as helpless victims of their circumstances. They can be prone to depression, discontentment, and anxiety, and they often refuse to accept help, as doing so may challenge their "victim" identity.

- **Borderline Witch:** The Borderline Witch subtype is characterized by high levels of aggression and a need for control. These individuals often react strongly to perceived slights or indiscretions, punishing those they believe have wronged them. They are prone to "borderline rage," which can manifest as the destruction of objects valued by those they feel wronged by.

They can also be quite manipulative, often engaging in black-and-white thinking and possibly favoring one family member or child over others. Their behavior can be intrusive and domineering, often leading loved ones to become withdrawn.

- **Borderline Hermit:** The Borderline Hermit subtype tends to be characterized by intense paranoia and suspicion, often seeing the world as a dangerous place. These individuals may have difficulty trusting others and may isolate themselves due to their belief that everyone is out to harm them. Often, these individuals have experienced severe trauma in their past, such as sexual abuse, which contributes to their worldview and behaviors.

It is important to note that that these categories are not definitive and that individuals with BPD can exhibit traits from multiple categories. These categories are tools for understanding and discussing the various ways BPD can present, rather than rigid classifications. People with BPD are unique individuals with their own histories and experiences, and their symptoms can change over time. Treatment, such as psychotherapy, is often tailored to the individual's specific needs and symptoms.

Now that we have reached the end of this chapter, let us review the key points once more:

In this chapter, we explored the different ways BPD can manifest itself in individuals. We also discussed the different subtypes of BPD, as identified by psychologists Theodore Millon and Dr. Christine Lawson.

Key Points:

Theodore Millon's framework identifies four types of BPD: Discouraged, Petulant, Impulsive, and Self-destructive Borderline.

- **Discouraged Borderline:** People with this type often display behaviors similar to those of people with depression and anxiety disorders, with a deep-rooted fear of abandonment.

- **Petulant Borderline:** Characterized by mood swings, passive-aggressive behavior, and defiance, these individuals often feel undeserving and angry.

- **Impulsive Borderline:** This type involves impulsive behaviors, risky activities, and quick mood swings. People with impulsive BPD may have a fear of abandonment and loss.

- **Self-destructive Borderline:** This type is characterized by a persistent feeling of inner turmoil and self-loathing, often resulting in harmful behaviors directed towards oneself.

Dr. Christine Lawson's subtypes of BPD, as proposed in her book "Understanding the Borderline Mother": Borderline Queen, Borderline Waif, Borderline Witch, and Borderline Hermit.

- **Borderline Queen:** These individuals are often perfectionistic and defensive, with an inability to accept criticism.

- **Borderline Waif:** Characterized as the "victim" subtype, these individuals often see themselves as helpless victims of their circumstances and are prone to depression and anxiety.

- **Borderline Witch:** This subtype is characterized by high levels of aggression and a need for control, often leading to manipulative and domineering behaviors.

- **Borderline Hermit:** These individuals often have intense paranoia and suspicion, frequently viewing the world as a dangerous place and isolating themselves as a result.

- It is important to remember that these categories are not definitive, and individuals with BPD can exhibit traits from multiple categories. Each individual with BPD is unique, and symptoms can change over time. Treatment is often tailored to the individual's specific needs and symptoms.

Now that we have explored the many faces of borderline personality disorder, we can move on to discover the different factors that can contribute to its development.

CHAPTER 5: THE ROOTS OF BORDERLINE PERSONALITY DISORDER: WHAT WE KNOW SO FAR

Could there be a hidden pattern behind the complexity of borderline personality disorder that we have yet to fully uncover?

While the exact cause of BPD is still unknown, researchers believe that it is likely caused by a combination of factors, including genetics, childhood trauma, and environmental factors. As we learn more about BPD, we may be able to identify the hidden pattern that underlies this complex disorder.

Several factors are believed to play a role in the development of borderline personality disorder. These include:

Genetics: we strive to fully understand the complex factors that contribute to borderline personality disorder, research has shown that genetics plays a role. **Heredity**, or the passing down of physical or mental characteristics from one generation to another, may seem simple at first. However, when it comes to mental health disorders like BPD, the picture is more complex. Studies have shown that people who have a parent or sibling with BPD are more likely to develop the disorder themselves. This is likely due to the fact that genes can influence the way the brain functions and processes emotions. **Identical twins** provide further evidence of a genetic link to BPD. If one identical twin has BPD, the other twin has a two-thirds chance of developing the disorder. This is because identical twins share 100% of their genes, while fraternal twins only share 50%. While the role of genetics in BPD is clear, the exact genes involved are still unknown. This is because BPD is a complex disorder that is likely caused by a combination of genetic and environmental factors. As research continues, we may be able to identify the specific genes that contribute to BPD. This could lead to new treatments that target these genes and help people with BPD live healthier and more fulfilling lives.

Issues with Chemicals in the Brain: In addition to the role of genetics, it seems that borderline personality disorder may be intricately intertwined with the brain's complex chemistry. Specifically, there is a growing body of evidence suggesting that certain irregularities in the brain's neurotransmitter system may contribute to the development of BPD. **Neurotransmitters** are chemical messengers that allow neurons, or brain cells, to communicate with each other. They play a pivotal role in our overall wellbeing, and are involved in a wide range of functions, including mood regulation, impulse control, and our perception of pain. Researchers believe that people with BPD may experience dysregulation in their neurotransmitter systems, particularly involving serotonin. Serotonin is often referred to as the "feel-good" neurotransmitter, and is involved in a number of functions, including mood regulation, impulse control, and our perception of pain. An imbalance or irregularity in serotonin levels, then, can have far-reaching effects. Several studies have shown a link between altered serotonin levels and symptoms associated with BPD, such as emotional instability, impulsivity, and intense, often explosive anger. Furthermore, low levels of serotonin are often found in individuals who experience depression, aggression, and self-destructive urges - symptoms that frequently present in people with BPD.

However, as with many aspects of mental health, the picture isn't black and white. While serotonin irregularities may play a role in BPD, it's important to remember that the brain is a complex organ with numerous interacting chemicals and systems. In other words, while an imbalance in serotonin may contribute to BPD symptoms, it's just one piece of a much larger and multifaceted puzzle.

The science behind neurotransmitter involvement in BPD is still unfolding. As researchers delve deeper into the labyrinth of the brain's biochemistry, we hope to gain a clearer understanding of these chemical messengers' role in BPD. Ultimately, the goal is to utilize this knowledge to develop more effective and personalized treatments for those living with this disorder.

Issues with Brain Development: Recent advancements in neuroimaging technology have enabled researchers to examine the brain structure and function in people with borderline personality disorder more closely. Their findings suggest that differences in certain regions of the brain may be implicated in BPD.

The brain is a complex organ, and different regions or **"districts"** perform specialized functions. Among those that have drawn particular interest in BPD research are:

- **The orbitofrontal cortex** is involved in decision-making, impulse control, and moderating social behavior. In people with BPD, researchers have noticed that this region may show atypical development or unusual activity patterns.

- **The hippocampus** is involved in a wide range of functions, including emotion regulation, memory formation, and controlling our responses to stress. It also helps us exert self-control and manage our behavior. In people with BPD, some studies have observed potential differences in the development or functioning of this area.

- **The amygdala** is involved in the processing and expression of emotions, especially negative emotions like fear, anxiety, and aggression. Studies indicate that people with BPD may have an amygdala that is unusually active or sensitive, potentially leading to heightened emotional reactivity and difficulty regulating intense emotional responses.

While these findings are intriguing, it is important to interpret them with caution. The brain is extraordinarily complex, and we are just beginning to understand how it works. It is also worth noting that these changes in brain structure and function may not be exclusive to BPD. They can also be found in other mental health disorders, suggesting that they might be related more generally to mental illness or stress.

Overall, these discoveries offer important insights into the biological basis of BPD. However, the precise role they play in the onset or maintenance of the disorder and whether they are a cause or consequence of the disorder remains to be fully understood. Nevertheless, these findings underscore the fact that BPD, like all mental health disorders, is a legitimate and complex condition with roots in both our biology and our experiences.

Environmental Factors: In addition to the complex interplay of genetics and brain function, the environment we grow up in, **the experiences we have, especially during our formative years**, significantly contribute to the development of Borderline Personality Disorder. This underlines the pervasive impact of childhood on our adult life, highlighting how early experiences can have far-reaching implications.

Some of the environmental influences commonly reported among individuals with BPD are:

- **Childhood Neglect:** It's a heart-wrenching reality that many people with BPD have experienced neglect during their childhood. Neglect can make a child feel unloved, unimportant, or invisible, shaping how they perceive themselves and their worth as they grow older.

- **Abuse:** Experiences of physical, emotional, or sexual

abuse, especially during childhood, are sadly prevalent in the histories of many individuals with BPD. Such traumatic experiences can significantly distort a person's self-image and their view of others and the world.

- **Chronic Fear or Stress:** Living in an environment of constant fear or stress, particularly during childhood, can create a sense of uncertainty and insecurity that extends into adulthood. This can contribute to the instability of self-image, relationships, and emotions often seen in BPD.

- **Exposure to Mental Illness or Substance Abuse in the Family:** Growing up with a family member who struggles with mental health issues or substance abuse can also contribute to the development of BPD. Living in such an environment can introduce a level of unpredictability and chaos that can be difficult for a child to process and cope with.

Childhood trauma, whether it's neglect, abuse, or prolonged exposure to fear or stress, **can leave deep psychological scars** that manifest in a myriad of ways in adult life. Some individuals might hide their authentic feelings and present a "false self" to the world, others might grapple with crippling feelings of low self-worth. Attachment issues often arise, leading to unhealthy patterns in relationships.

In the context of BPD, the impact of childhood trauma may be reflected in a deep-seated expectation of abandonment, a tendency to idealize or demonize others, or an anticipation of being mistreated. It's like a haunting echo from the past, shaping perceptions, expectations, and interactions in the present.

However, it's crucial to remember that having these experiences doesn't guarantee the development of BPD. People are incredibly resilient, and many who endure such circumstances do not develop the disorder. Conversely, some people with BPD may not have these experiences in their history. The complexity of this condition suggests that it is caused by multiple factors, including genetic, biological, and environmental factors. Understanding this complexity is essential for reducing the stigma associated with this condition and promoting empathy, compassion, and effective treatment strategies.

We have explored the many causes of this condition in depth. Let's take a moment to review before we move on:

Borderline personality disorder is a complex mental health condition that is believed to be caused by a combination of factors, including genetics, brain chemistry, and environmental influences.

Key Points:

- **Genetics:** There is a strong genetic component to

BPD, meaning that people who have a family history of the disorder are more likely to develop it themselves. However, the exact genes involved are still unknown.

- **Brain Chemistry:** Imbalances in brain chemicals, particularly the neurotransmitter serotonin, may also contribute to BPD. Serotonin is involved in regulating mood, impulse control, and social behavior. People with BPD often have low levels of serotonin, which can lead to emotional instability, impulsivity, and intense anger.

- **Environmental Influences:** Adverse childhood experiences, such as neglect, abuse, or exposure to chronic fear and stress, can also play a role in the development of BPD. These experiences can damage the developing brain and lead to problems with self-regulation, emotional stability, and relationships.

- **It's important to remember that BPD is a complex disorder, and there is no single cause.** A combination of genetic, biological, and environmental factors likely contribute to its development.

Now that we have explored the complex factors that can lead to this condition, we will discuss diagnosis in the following pages.

CHAPTER 6: THE DIAGNOSTIC CRITERIA FOR BORDERLINE PERSONALITY DISORDER

Did you know that borderline personality disorder affects between **1.6%** and **5.9%** of the general population, but is often unrecognized or misdiagnosed?

This is because the disorder is complex and its symptoms overlap with other mental health conditions. As a result, people with BPD may receive inappropriate treatments.

This is a startling fact that highlights the need for improved recognition and understanding of BPD in the mental health field. With better understanding, clinicians can more accurately diagnose BPD and provide appropriate treatment. This can improve the lives of people with BPD and help them to live healthier, happier lives.

In the previous chapters, we explored the complex nature of borderline personality disorder. One thing that became clear is that BPD is a condition that requires professional guidance. It is not something that can be navigated alone.

BPD is a whirlwind of emotions that can escalate into violence, damage relationships, and lead to harmful behaviors. In the most tragic cases, it can lead to suicide.

It is important to remember that you do not have to go through this alone. There are professionals who have been trained to provide the support, guidance, and treatment necessary to manage and potentially overcome BPD.

If you or someone you know is struggling with BPD, please reach out for help. There is no shame in seeking professional help. In fact, it is one of the most important things you can do for yourself.

Questions that you can ask yourself during a self-assessment:

- Do you notice a rapid shifting in your emotional state, with moods changing like the wind?

- Do you find yourself frequently immersed in extreme emotions, such as intense anger, profound sadness, or deep-seated distress?

- Does an unshakeable sense of emptiness or dissatisfaction seem to hang over you, becoming a constant companion?

- Is the fear of abandonment a persistent worry, haunting you with the thought of losing those you care about?

- Would you describe your romantic relationships as a roller coaster ride, veering between heightened intensity and troubling instability?

- Do you find your perception of people close to you oscillating wildly from one extreme to another, with little middle ground?

- Have you found yourself at the edge, considering self-harm or suicide, driven by unbearable emotional turmoil?

- When faced with insecurities in a relationship, do you often resort to impulsive reactions or intense behaviors in a frantic effort to keep your partner anchored to you?

- Have you found yourself occasionally embarking on risky exploits, such as binge drinking, drug abuse, unsafe sexual practices, or reckless driving?

If you or a loved one find yourselves resonating with several, or all, of these inquiries, it might suggest the presence of Borderline Personality Disorder. However, bear in mind that self-assessment is just an initial step. It's essential to remember that self-diagnosis comes with a fair share of limitations. The nuances of mental health diagnosis require the expertise and guidance of a professional. Therefore, seeking help from a qualified mental health professional for a proper diagnosis and treatment plan is of utmost importance.

Professional Diagnosis Process

The professional diagnosis of BPD is usually made by a highly trained mental health specialist, such as a psychiatrist or clinical psychologist. The diagnosis process involves several steps:

- **Clinical interview:** The mental health professional will conduct a detailed discussion about your symptoms, including when they started, how they affect your life, and if you have any thoughts of self-harm or suicide. They will also ask about your personal and family medical history.

- **Psychiatric evaluation:** The mental health professional will evaluate your thought patterns, feelings, and behavioral tendencies. They will use this information to determine if you meet the diagnostic criteria for BPD.

- **Diagnostic criteria:** *The American Psychiatric Association's Diagnostic and Statistical Manual of Mental Disorders* (DSM-5) lists nine specific symptoms that are characteristic of BPD. To be diagnosed with BPD, you must have experienced at least five of these symptoms for a significant period of time.

- **Physical examination and lab tests:** BPD cannot be diagnosed through laboratory tests or imaging, but your healthcare provider may recommend a physical examination or specific tests to rule out other medical conditions that may be causing your symptoms.

- **Observation of behavior patterns:** The mental health professional will observe your behavior patterns over time. Individuals with BPD typically exhibit recurring patterns of intense and fluctuating relationships, emotional instability, and impulsivity. Recognizing these patterns can provide further confirmation of a BPD diagnosis.

- **Evaluation of co-occurring disorders:** It is common for individuals with BPD to have other mental health conditions, such as depression, anxiety disorders, eating disorders, or substance misuse. The mental health professional will evaluate these co-occurring conditions to develop an effective treatment plan.

Once a diagnosis is made, a comprehensive and individualized treatment plan will be created. This plan may include psychotherapy, medication, and self-care strategies.

The diagnosis process for BPD can be lengthy and intensive, but it is important to ensure an accurate diagnosis so that you can receive the most effective treatment.

Before moving on to the next chapter, let us take a moment to reflect on what we have been saying.

In this chapter, we discussed the causes and diagnostic process of borderline personality disorder, shedding light on its complexities and the necessity for professional intervention.

- BPD is a complex mental health condition that affects between 1.6% and 5.9% of the general population.

- BPD is often unrecognized or misdiagnosed due to its complexity and overlapping symptoms with other mental health conditions.

- There is no single cause of BPD, but it is thought to be caused by a combination of genetic, environmental, and psychological factors.

- The diagnostic process for BPD is complex and can take several months or even years to complete.

- There is no cure for BPD, but it can be managed with a combination of psychotherapy, medication, and self-care strategies.

If you or someone you know is struggling with BPD, it is important to seek professional help. There are many resources available to help people with BPD live healthy and fulfilling lives.

Self-assessment

- Do you have a fear of abandonment?

- Do you have intense mood swings?

- Do you have unstable relationships?

- Do you have a history of self-harm or suicidal thoughts?

- Do you have difficulty controlling your emotions?

- Do you have a distorted sense of self?

If you answered yes to any of these questions, it is important to talk to a mental health professional. They can help you assess your symptoms and develop a treatment plan.

The professional diagnostic process for BPD typically includes the following steps:

- Clinical interview: The mental health professional will conduct a detailed interview about your symptoms, including when they started, how they affect your life, and if you have any thoughts of self-harm or suicide.

- Psychiatric evaluation: The mental health professional will evaluate your thought patterns, feelings, and behavioral tendencies.

- Assessment based on DSM-5 diagnostic criteria: The mental health professional will assess your symptoms based on the diagnostic criteria for BPD in the *Diagnostic and Statistical Manual of Mental Disorders*.

- Physical examinations and lab tests: The mental health professional may recommend physical examinations and lab tests to rule out other medical conditions that may be causing your symptoms.

- Observation of behavioral patterns: The mental health professional will observe your behavior patterns over time.

- Evaluation of co-occurring disorders: The mental health professional will evaluate any co-occurring mental health conditions, such as depression, anxiety, or substance abuse.

So, what does a diagnosis of BPD mean for you or a loved one? Without a doubt, BPD presents a myriad of challenges that can impact not only the individual but also their relationships and overall quality of life. However, a diagnosis is not a death sentence, nor is it an indication of a lost cause. In fact, it marks the first step in understanding and managing this complex condition.

In the following chapters, we will explore strategies to navigate the journey of living with BPD, such as fostering resilience, creating supportive environments, and building healthy relationships. With appropriate support and care, it is entirely possible to lead a fulfilling and meaningful life despite a BPD diagnosis.

CHAPTER 7: WHAT TO EXPECT AFTER A BPD DIAGNOSIS

Have you recently been diagnosed with Borderline Personality Disorder?

A diagnosis of Borderline Personality Disorder can be jarring, clarifying, or both. It can stir a tumult of emotions, from relief to despair. BPD infiltrates every facet of your existence, influencing your self-perception, relationships, work, and leisure. The impulsive and sometimes violent tendencies characteristic of BPD can cause physical and emotional distress for you and those around you.

Navigating life with BPD requires understanding. With knowledge of your condition, you can brace for challenges, devise coping strategies, and manage turbulent emotions. You can also communicate effectively with loved ones about BPD, empowering them to support you.

With a BPD diagnosis, you may find yourself experiencing a range of intense emotions, including:

- Intense emotions and rapid mood swings that can feel overwhelming.

- Feelings of isolation and loneliness.

- A sense of being fundamentally defective.

- A belief that everything bad that happens is their fault.

- Confusion about their life's desires, preferences, and dislikes.

- A belief that they are a "bad person".

- A sense of being an imposter or not a "real" person.

- Feeling trapped in a grown-up's world while feeling like a child inside.

- Uncertainty about their identity.

- A sense of emptiness or a void.

These negative self-perceptions can lead to reactive behaviors, such as:

- Keeping themselves constantly busy to avoid confronting their thoughts.

- Frequently changing plans, hobbies, or jobs in the quest to find their true self.

- Engaging in impulsive behaviors, such as overspending or binge eating.

- Using recreational drugs or smoking.

- Drinking alcohol excessively to suppress their turbulent emotions.

- Avoiding commitment or seeing tasks through to completion.

- Avoiding any activities where failure or disappointment might be an outcome.

People with borderline personality disorder may experience intense emotions and difficulty regulating their emotions. These symptoms can have a significant impact on their relationships. For example, people with BPD may:

- Feel isolated, misunderstood, and unlike anyone

around them.

- View the world as a hostile place they'd prefer to escape from.

- Perceive people as either wholly perfect or irredeemably bad, with no in-between.

- Fear that any conflict could lead their loved ones to abandon them permanently.

These feelings can manifest in the following behaviors:

- Easily become frustrated and angry with people around them.

- Find it difficult to trust others, even those they love.

- Crave closeness, yet push people away out of fear they'll abandon them.

- Have unrealistically high expectations of friends and loved ones.

- Prematurely end relationships if they fear the other person might leave them.

- Constantly be on the lookout for signs of impending abandonment in their relationships.

We recognize that receiving a diagnosis of BPD can have a significant impact on an individual's life. Let's take a moment to review the key points we discussed in this chapter:

Key Points:

- **Emotions:** Receiving a diagnosis of BPD can be a very emotional experience, with people feeling a range of intense emotions, including relief, despair, and a sense of being fundamentally flawed.

- **Self-perceptions:** People with BPD may also experience negative self-perceptions, such as viewing themselves as defective, believing they are to blame for all bad occurrences, feeling like imposters, and experiencing confusion about their identity and life desires.

- **Coping strategies:** In an effort to cope with these difficult emotions and perceptions, people with BPD may resort to a variety of coping strategies, including staying constantly busy, frequently changing plans or jobs, engaging in impulsive behaviors, and avoiding commitment.

- **Relationships:** BPD can also have a significant impact on relationships. People with BPD may find it difficult to trust others, may fear abandonment, and may view others as either completely perfect or irredeemably bad.

- **Behaviors:** As a result of these emotions, perceptions, and coping strategies, people with BPD may exhibit a variety of behaviors, such as getting easily frustrated, pushing people away, and prematurely ending relationships due to the fear of being left.

In the following chapters, we will explore a variety of strategies and techniques for managing BPD. Although the road to recovery will not be easy, there is hope. With perseverance, patience, and the support of a therapist, many people with BPD have successfully transformed their lives. You can be one of them.

Remember, you are not your disorder. It is a part of your life, but it does not define you or your potential. Let's begin our journey to better understand and manage BPD, so we can create a more fulfilling and successful future.

CHAPTER 8: COPING WITH THE EMOTIONAL ROLLERCOSTER

Have you ever felt helpless and out of control in the midst of an intense swirl of emotions?

This is a common experience for people with borderline personality disorder. The hallmark of BPD is often this torrent of overwhelming emotions, which can seem impossible to manage. But there is hope.

While you may feel lost in the eye of this tempest, there are strategies you can use to steer through it. When you're calm, take the time to explore and understand these techniques. Having a tailored action plan ready for when the emotional waves surge again can provide you with a sense of control and reassurance when your emotions seem to spiral out of control.

In the following paragraphs, we will explore a variety of strategies that can be helpful in weathering emotional storms. These include:

Recognizing Your Emotions

Recognizing your emotions is the first step to managing them. When you have BPD, it can be difficult to identify your emotions because you may be experiencing a whirlwind of contradictory emotions at once. This can be like being tossed on a stormy sea.

If you find yourself feeling overwhelmed, try to take things one minute at a time. Breaking the situation down into smaller steps can make it seem more manageable. Also, focus on identifying one emotion at a time. Can you label your feeling? Is it anger, frustration, excitement, or sadness? Try to identify the emotion without trying to figure out why you're feeling it or how to stop feeling it.

Here are some physical indicators that can help you identify your emotions:

Anger

When you're angry, your body goes into "fight or flight" mode. This is a natural response to a perceived threat. Your body releases stress hormones, such as cortisol and adrenaline, which cause a number of physical changes, including:

- **Increased heart rate:** Your heart rate increases to pump more blood to your muscles, preparing you for action.

- **Faster breathing:** Your breathing becomes faster to bring more oxygen into your body.

- **Muscle tension:** Your muscles tense up, ready for physical exertion.

- **Restlessness:** You may feel fidgety or restless, unable to sit still.

- **Clenched fists or jaw:** You may clench your fists or jaw, as a way of releasing pent-up energy.

Grief

Grief is a natural response to loss. When you grieve, your body may experience a number of physical symptoms, including:

- **Chest pain:** You may feel a physical ache in your chest, as though your heart is literally heavy with sorrow.

- **Loss of appetite:** You may find that you don't have much of an appetite, or that food just doesn't taste the same.

- **Fatigue:** You may feel tired all the time, as your body and mind cope with the emotional pain.

- **Trouble sleeping:** You may find it difficult to fall asleep or stay asleep, as your mind revisits your loss during quiet moments.

Anxiety

Anxiety is a feeling of worry, nervousness, or unease. When you're anxious, your body goes into "fight or flight" mode, even if there is no real threat present. This can cause a number of physical symptoms, including:

- **Sweating:** You may start to sweat, even if you're not hot.

- **Widened pupils:** Your pupils may dilate, allowing more light into your eyes.

- **Muscle tension:** Your muscles may tense up, making you feel stiff or sore.

- **Hot flashes or chills:** You may experience hot flashes or chills, as your body temperature fluctuates.

- **Chest pain:** You may feel a tightness or pain in your

chest.

- **Shortness of breath:** You may find it difficult to breathe, or that your breathing is shallow.

- **Dry mouth:** Your mouth may feel dry, as your body produces less saliva.

- **Nausea:** You may feel nauseous, or like you might vomit.

- **Tingling sensations:** You may feel tingling sensations in your hands, feet, or other parts of your body.

It's important to remember that everyone experiences these emotions differently. What works for one person may not work for another. The most important thing is to find what works for you and to be patient with yourself.

Welcoming Your Emotions

Identifying your emotions is the first step, but the true challenge lies in wholeheartedly embracing them. This acceptance is a key part of taming the emotional tempest within. It may seem like an insurmountable challenge, especially if you have been grappling with the disruptive effects of borderline personality disorder for a considerable period. The resentment you harbor towards the disorder and the associated emotions can make the prospect of acceptance feel overwhelming.

However, it is important to understand that acceptance does not equate to approval or resignation. When you accept your emotions, you are not justifying them or conceding to their permanence. Rather, acceptance involves relinquishing the habitual instinct to dismiss or suppress these feelings. By allowing yourself the space to genuinely experience your emotions instead of constantly battling against them, you can significantly diminish their control over you.

Make a conscious effort to allow your emotions to exist without sinking into the mire of self-criticism or self-judgment. Aim to stay in the present moment, resisting the lure of past regrets or future anxieties.

Here are some techniques you might find helpful:

- **Adopt the role of an external observer to your emotions.** Keep in mind that your emotions do not define you. You are not the anger, the grief, the frustration, or the anxiety you feel. Endeavor to view your emotions as what they truly are - transient states that are separate from the core essence of who you are.

- **Take note of the natural rhythm of your emotions.** Picture them as waves in the ocean - they rise and fall, intensify and wane. This imagery can fortify your understanding that your emotions are not intrinsic components of your identity but temporary states that fluctuate.

- **Tune into your physical sensations.** How are your emotions expressed physically within you? Do you sense tension or pain? If so, where is it located? Does this discomfort change along with the intensity of your feelings? Strive to identify where you physically feel the impact of your emotions and describe the sensation. Could it be described as a dull ache? A piercing pain? A burning sensation? A tingling?

- **Offer yourself reassurances that it's perfectly okay to experience these emotions.** Welcome them for what they are, without any judgment. Remember, accepting these feelings doesn't suggest that you approve of them or that they are permanent.

- **Gently remind yourself that your current emotions are not a mirror of your reality.** They are the by-products of your thoughts, and thoughts, by their very nature, can be altered. Emotions are ephemeral - they come and go. Just because you're feeling a particular way right now, doesn't solidify that you'll always feel this way.

Immerse in Mindfulness Practices

Mindfulness is a type of meditation that can help you to better understand and manage your thoughts and emotions. It has been shown to be effective in treating a variety of mental health conditions, including borderline personality disorder.

There are many different ways to practice mindfulness. Some common techniques include:

- **Traditional mindfulness meditation:** This involves focusing on your breath. Notice the flow of your breath as it moves in and out of your body, and tune into its rhythm. When you observe thoughts emerging, merely acknowledge them, and then visualize them drifting away on an imaginary river. You can achieve a similar effect by concentrating on a mantra (a phrase repeated) instead of your breath.

- **Sensory mindfulness meditation:** Here, you pay attention to each of your senses. Identify five things you can see, hear, smell, touch, and taste. Challenge yourself to describe these sensory experiences in great detail. For instance, instead of merely saying, "I see a butterfly," elaborate on your observation: "I see a butterfly with dark yellow wings, dotted with small semi-circular black spots. Its legs are rhythmically moving in a slow back-and-forth motion." Apply the same level of detail to descriptions of things you hear, smell, feel, and taste. This technique is excellent for anchoring yourself in the present moment and diverting focus from the past or future.

- **Bodied sensation mindfulness:** Close your eyes and become conscious of the subtle sensations within your body. Do you feel an itch? A dull ache? A tingling? Instead of resisting these sensations, simply acknowledge them and allow them to pass. Begin from the top of your head and work your way down to the tips of your toes, mentally scanning every part of your body. Note what you observe, providing the same depth of description you would in a sensory meditation.

- **Emotional mindfulness:** This approach requires you to permit and accept arising emotions without judgment. Instead of combating your emotions, attempt to label them. What are you feeling? Anger? Jealousy? Frustration? Happiness? Whatever it is, accept it, then let it go. Picture your emotion floating away on a river, similar to how you would let go of a distracting thought during traditional mindfulness meditation.

Mastering Impulse Control

People with borderline personality disorder often struggle with impulsive urges. These urges can lead to reckless, self-destructive behaviors, such as self-harm, dangerous driving, and unsafe sex. Even though you know these behaviors are harmful, they can feel like the only way to cope with emotional distress.

It is possible to manage impulsive urges. The first step is to recognize that these behaviors serve a purpose. **They are coping mechanisms that help you deal with distress.** It is important to view them in this light, rather than as reasons for self-punishment.

However, it is also important to remember that **these behaviors can be harmful to you and others.** It is essential to find healthier, less destructive ways to cope with distress.

One way to do this is to learn to tolerate distress. This means learning to sit with your emotions without immediately trying to escape them. When you feel an urge to act impulsively, take a few deep breaths and try to calm down. Once you have calmed down, you can start to think about healthier ways to cope with your emotions.

Indeed, managing distress can seem much simpler in theory than it actually is in practice. However, there are a few strategies you can apply to start developing your tolerance to distress.

Regulating Your Body Temperature

When you feel angry or frustrated, your body temperature often rises. This is a natural response to stress. However, if your body temperature gets too high, it can make it difficult to think clearly and to control your emotions.

There are a few things you can do to regulate your body temperature and to calm down.

- **Splash cold water on your face:** This will help to lower your body temperature and to reduce feelings of anger or frustration.

- **Stand in front of a fan or air conditioner:** This will also help to lower your body temperature.

- **Step outside if you're in a warm environment:** This will help you to cool down and to clear your head.

Incorporate Intense Exercise

When you are feeling overwhelmed by intense emotions, engaging in high-intensity exercise can be a powerful way to manage your distress. Exercise increases oxygen flow to the brain, which can help to improve mood and reduce stress. Additionally, the physical exhaustion from vigorous activity can make it less likely that you will engage in harmful or reckless behaviors.

Here are some examples of high-intensity exercises that you can try:

- Running

- Swimming

- Spot-running

- HIIT (high-intensity interval training)

If you are new to exercise, start slowly and gradually increase the intensity and duration of your workouts. It is also important to listen to your body and rest when you need to.

Exercise is a safe and effective way to manage intense emotions.

Practice Mindful Breathing

Mindful breathing is a technique that can be used to manage distress. It involves focusing your attention on your breath and deliberately regulating your breathing to a steady rhythm.

To practice mindful breathing, find a quiet place where you will not be disturbed. Sit or lie down in a comfortable position. Close your eyes and take a few deep breaths. Notice the natural rise and fall of your chest and abdomen.

Once you have found a steady rhythm, begin to count your breaths. Inhale for a count of five, hold for a count of two, and exhale for a count of five. Repeat this pattern for several minutes.

As you breathe, focus your attention on the sensations in your body. Notice the feeling of the air as it enters and leaves your lungs. Pay attention to any thoughts or feelings that arise. Do not judge or analyze these thoughts or feelings. Simply observe them and let them go.

Mindful breathing can help you to calm down and to focus your attention on the present moment. It can also help you to manage stress and to cope with difficult emotions.

Practice Progressive Muscle Relaxation

Progressive muscle relaxation (PMR) is a technique that can be used to reduce stress and tension. It involves tensing and then relaxing different muscle groups in the body.

To practice PMR, find a quiet place where you will not be disturbed. Sit or lie down in a comfortable position. Close your eyes and take a few deep breaths.

Once you are relaxed, begin to tense and relax different muscle groups in your body. Start with your toes. Tighten your toes as hard as you can for a count of five, and then relax them.

Repeat this process with your feet, calves, thighs, abdomen, chest, shoulders, arms, hands, face, and scalp.

As you tense and relax each muscle group, pay attention to the difference between the feeling of tension and the feeling of relaxation. Notice how your muscles feel when they are tense, and how they feel when they are relaxed.

Continue practicing PMR for 10-15 minutes. You may find it helpful to listen to relaxing music or to focus on a calming image as you practice.

PMR is a simple but effective technique that can be used to reduce stress and tension. It can be practiced daily, and the benefits will usually become apparent after a few weeks of regular practice.

Indulge in Soothing Activities

When you are feeling distressed, it is important to engage in activities that will help you to calm down. These activities should be healthy and safe, and they should help you to divert your attention from your distress.

Here are some examples of soothing activities:

- **Take a walk in nature:** Being in nature can help to reduce stress and anxiety.

- **Read a good book:** Reading can help you to relax and escape from your troubles.

- **Listen to your favorite music:** Listening to music can help to soothe your emotions.

- **Play a musical instrument:** Playing a musical instrument can help you to express your emotions in a healthy way.

- **Participate in a sport:** Exercise can help to reduce stress and improve your mood.

- **Gardening:** Gardening can be a relaxing and rewarding activity.

- **Painting:** Painting can help you to express your creativity and to relax your mind.

- **Bake a cake:** Baking can be a fun and therapeutic activity.

It is important to find activities that you enjoy and that will help you to relax. You may also find it helpful to create a list of soothing activities that you can refer to when you are feeling distressed.

Soothing activities are a form of self-care. When you engage in these activities, you are taking care of yourself and your mental health. Regularly practicing self-care can help you to manage your BPD symptoms and to improve your overall mood and wellbeing.

Engaging in Acts of Kindness

When you are feeling distressed, it can be helpful to engage in acts of kindness. Helping others can help to take your mind off of your own problems and can also make you feel good about yourself.

There are many different ways to engage in acts of kindness. Here are a few ideas:

- **Volunteer your time to a local charity.**

- **Help out a neighbor or friend with a task.**

- **Donate to a cause you care about.**

- **Be kind to animals.**

- **Smile at strangers.**

Even small acts of kindness can make a difference. When you help others, you are not only making them feel good, but you are also making yourself feel good.

If you are struggling with BPD, engaging in acts of kindness can be a helpful way to manage your symptoms. It can help you to feel more connected to others, more positive, and more in control of your emotions.

If you are not sure where to start, you can talk to your therapist or counselor for ideas. They can help you to find ways to engage in acts of kindness that are meaningful to you.

Keeping Your Mind Occupied

When you are feeling distressed, it can be helpful to keep your mind occupied. This can help to distract you from your negative thoughts and emotions.

There are many different activities that you can do to keep your mind occupied. Here are a few ideas:

- **Recite the alphabet backward.**

- **Do mental arithmetic.**

- **Play a game of chess.**

- **Solve a crossword or Sudoku puzzle.**

- **Write in a journal.**

- **Read a book.**

- **Listen to music.**

- **Take a walk.**

- **Do some yoga or meditation.**

The key is to find an activity that you enjoy and that will keep your mind occupied without causing you additional stress or frustration.

By keeping your mind occupied, you can effectively disrupt the cyclical pattern of distressing thoughts. This can provide you with a much-needed respite from your negative emotions.

Leverage the Power of Positive Visualization

Visualization is a powerful tool that can help you to manage distress. When you visualize yourself responding to a distressing situation in a positive way, you are essentially training your brain to react in that way when the situation actually arises.

To practice visualization, find a quiet place where you will not be disturbed. Close your eyes and take a few deep breaths. Once you are relaxed, imagine yourself in a distressing situation. What are you feeling? What are you thinking? How are you reacting?

Now, imagine yourself responding to the situation in a positive way. What are you doing differently? How are you feeling? How are you thinking?

Continue visualizing yourself responding in a positive way until you feel confident that you can do it in real life.

You can practice visualization whenever you feel stressed or anxious. The more you practice, the more effective it will become.

Assigning Positive Significance to Your Experiences

Every experience, even those associated with distress or impulsive behavior, can be an opportunity for growth and learning. By consciously seeking out the positive aspects of your experiences, you can reframe your understanding of distressing situations.

Here are some ways to assign positive significance to your experiences:

- **Consider how grappling with your distress may be fortifying your resilience.** Every time you face distress and come out on the other side, you are building your mental and emotional stamina. This accumulated strength can bolster your confidence to face similar situations in the future.

- **Reflect on the lessons you've learned from past situations.** Have your experiences taught you about certain triggers to avoid, or better ways to respond to emotional upheavals? Even in the most difficult times, there is often wisdom to be found.

- **Evaluate the relationships and connections that might have developed as a result of your experiences.** Have you found support from unexpected places? Perhaps a certain crisis led you to connect with someone who proved to be a valuable friend or ally.

- **Consider how your experiences have made you a more compassionate and understanding person.** Overcoming challenges can often lead to increased empathy and understanding for others in similar situations. You might find that your experiences with BPD enable you to provide support and encouragement to others who are struggling with their own mental health issues.

By consciously assigning positive meaning to your experiences, you can shift your perspective from one of suffering to one of growth and resilience. This practice can help you feel more in control of your emotions, more resilient in the face of distress, and more optimistic about the future.

Adopt a Balanced Perspective: Using a Pros and Cons List

When you are feeling impulsive, it can be helpful to create a pros and cons list to help you make a more informed decision.

Here are the steps on how to create a pros and cons list:

1. **Identify the impulsive behavior.** What impulsive behavior are you considering? For example, it could be engaging in substance abuse, overspending, acting out in anger, or engaging in risky sexual behavior.

2. **List the pros and cons.** On one side of the list, write down the pros or immediate benefits of the behavior. On the other side of the list, write down the cons or potential negative consequences.

3. **Evaluate the list.** Once you have written down the pros and cons, take a moment to step back and objectively review what you have written. Try to identify any patterns, key insights, or strong arguments that stand out to you.

4. **Make a decision.** Now that you have laid out the potential advantages and disadvantages, you are better equipped to make a decision. Remember that the goal is not necessarily to have more pros or cons, but to fully understand the potential implications of your impulsive behavior.

Creating a pros and cons list can help you slow down and distance yourself from the intensity of your emotions. This can give you the time and space you need to make healthier decisions, instead of acting on impulse.

We have covered a lot of ground in this chapter on managing out-of-control emotions. It has been a dense and information-rich chapter, so let's take a moment to reflect on what we have learned:

When you're feeling overwhelmed by your emotions, it can be helpful to break things down into smaller steps. This can make the situation seem less daunting and help you feel more in control.

Try to identify and label one emotion at a time. Don't worry about trying to analyze why you're feeling it or how to stop feeling it. Just focus on recognizing what you're feeling.

Physical sensations can often help you identify your emotions. For example, anger can cause your heart rate to increase, your breathing to become faster, and your muscles to tense up. Grief can cause chest pain, a loss of appetite, fatigue, and trouble sleeping. Anxiety can cause sweating, widened pupils, muscle tension, hot flashes or chills, chest pain, shortness of breath, a dry mouth, nausea, and tingling sensations.

Once you've identified your emotions, you can start to welcome them. This doesn't mean you have to like them or agree with them. It just means accepting them for what they are. Emotions are a normal part of life, and they're not going to go away. The sooner you accept them, the sooner you can start to move on.

Key Points:

Here are some techniques that can help you welcome your emotions:

- **Adopt the role of an external observer.** Imagine you're watching yourself from a distance. This can help you see your emotions from a different perspective and make them seem less overwhelming.

- **Note the natural rhythm of your emotions.** Emotions fluctuate over time, just like waves in the ocean. Remind yourself that this is normal and that your emotions will pass.

- **Tune into your physical sensations.** Pay attention to how your body reacts to different emotions. This can help you understand your emotions better and make them seem less scary.

- **Offer yourself reassurances.** Remind yourself that it's okay to feel these emotions. You're not alone, and you're not going crazy.

It's important to remember that your emotions are not a direct reflection of reality. They are the by-products of your thoughts, which can change over time.

Here are some other coping strategies that can help you manage your emotions:

- **Practice mindfulness.** Mindfulness is the practice of paying attention to the present moment without judgment. It can help you ground yourself and create a sense of calm amidst emotional turmoil.

- **Employ cognitive distractions.** Engaging in activities that require concentration can help distract you from overwhelming emotions. This could include reading, listening to music, or playing a game.

- **Use positive imagery.** Envisioning calming or happy scenarios can help shift your emotional state. This could involve imagining yourself on a beach, taking a walk in the woods, or spending time with loved ones.

- **Give meaning to the situation.** Try to find a lesson or a positive aspect in challenging situations. This can help you shift your perspective and make it easier to cope with your emotions.

- **Make a pros and cons list.** When faced with a difficult decision, listing out the pros and cons can help clarify your thoughts and emotions related to the situation.

These are just a few strategies that can help you manage your emotions. What works for one person might not work for another. The important thing is to find what strategies work best for you.

I hope this chapter has been helpful. In the next chapter, we'll cover who can provide you with the professional help you need. You're not alone, and there are qualified people who want to support you.

CHAPTER 9: THE IMPORTANCE OF A SUPPORT SYSTEM IN BPD RECOVERY

Have you ever felt lost in your own emotions? Like you're the only one who knows what it's like to feel so much, all the time? If you have borderline personality disorder, you're not alone.

BPD is a mental health condition that can make it hard to manage your emotions. You might feel intense anger, sadness, or anxiety. You might have trouble controlling your impulses. And you might have a hard time maintaining relationships.

But there is hope. There are treatments that can help you manage your symptoms and live a full and meaningful life.

One of the most important things you can do is to build a strong support network. This could include your family, friends, therapist, or other mental health professionals.

Your loved ones can offer you love, support, and understanding. They can help you stay on track with your treatment and remind you that you're not alone.

Your therapist can teach you coping skills and help you understand your disorder. They can also provide you with a safe space to talk about your feelings.

There are also many online and in-person support groups for people with BPD. These groups can provide you with a sense of community and give you the opportunity to connect with others who understand what you're going through.

Remember, you're not alone. BPD is a treatable condition, and there are people who want to help. With the right support, you can live a happy and fulfilling life.

Navigating the Path to Your Perfect Mental Health Care Professional

Finding a therapist who can help you manage borderline personality disorder can be a daunting task. But it's important to remember that you're not alone. Your primary care provider can help you get started, and there are many resources available to help you find the right therapist for you.

Here are a few things to keep in mind when searching for a therapist:

- Expertise: Make sure the therapist you choose has experience working with people with BPD. This is an important factor, as BPD can be a complex disorder that requires specialized treatment.

- Location: Consider your location when searching for a therapist. If you prefer to see a therapist in person, you'll need to find someone who is close to you. If you're open to seeing a therapist online, you'll have a wider range of options.

- Cost: Therapy can be expensive, so it's important to factor in the cost when making your decision. Some therapists offer sliding scale fees or payment plans, so be sure to ask about financial assistance.

- Personality: It's important to feel comfortable with your therapist. You'll be sharing a lot of personal information with them, so it's important to find someone you can trust and relate to.

Once you've found a few potential therapists, it's a good idea to schedule a free consultation. This will give you a chance to meet the therapist and see if they're a good fit for you.

When you're looking for a therapist to help you with Borderline Personality Disorder, it's important to feel comfortable and confident in their ability to help you. Here are some questions you might want to ask to get a better sense of their approach to treatment:

- **Do you have experience treating people with BPD?** If so, what have your experiences been like?

- **What is your approach to treating BPD?** What types of therapy do you use?

- **How do you help people manage their emotions?** What techniques do you use?

- **How do you help people develop healthy relationships?** What tools do you provide?

- **How do you help people with self-harm or suicidal thoughts?** What resources do you offer?

- **What are your fees?** Do you accept my insurance?

It's also important to feel like you can be open and honest with your therapist. If you're not comfortable sharing your thoughts and feelings, it will be difficult to make progress in treatment. So be sure to ask about their confidentiality policies and what you can expect in terms of feedback and support.

Steps to Enhance Your Success in Overcoming BPD

Overcoming Borderline Personality Disorder necessitates a proactive approach to your own treatment. Relying solely on your psychologist or other healthcare provider may not suffice in managing the emotional turbulence that comes with the disorder. Therefore, embracing the steps outlined below can significantly augment your chances of successful treatment:

Here are some additional tips that may help you in your recovery from BPD:

- **Take care of your physical health:** Eating a healthy diet, exercising regularly, and getting enough sleep are all important for your overall well-being. When you feel good physically, you are better able to manage your emotional symptoms.

- **Practice mindfulness and relaxation techniques:** Mindfulness is the practice of paying attention to the present moment without judgment. Relaxation techniques such as yoga, meditation, or deep breathing can help you calm down and reduce stress.

- **Stay connected with your support system:** Talk to your friends and family about what you are going through. They can offer emotional support and help you stay grounded. You may also want to consider joining a support group for people with BPD.

- **Avoid triggers:** Pay attention to the things that make your symptoms worse. Once you know what your triggers are, you can start to avoid them or develop strategies for coping with them.

- **Stay organized:** Keeping your life organized can help reduce stress and anxiety. This may include setting up a daily routine, keeping track of appointments, and organizing your belongings.

- **Take small steps each day:** Don't expect to change overnight. Set small, achievable goals for yourself and celebrate your successes along the way.

- **Don't lose hope:** Recovery from BPD is possible. It takes time and effort, but it is worth it. Remember that you are not alone and there are people who care about you and want to help.

- **Keep a journal:** Writing down your thoughts, feelings, and experiences can help you track your progress and identify patterns. It can also be a helpful way to express your emotions and cope with difficult situations.

Understanding Recovery Expectations

Recovering from a physical illness is often a straightforward process that involves getting better from being unwell. However, recovery from a mental illness like Borderline Personality Disorder can be more complex. While it is possible to make significant progress in managing BPD symptoms, it is important to remember that recovery is not always a linear process.

There are many different ways to measure progress in BPD recovery. Some common indicators of improvement include:

- **Decreased frequency and intensity of emotional outbursts:** When you are on the road to recovery, you may notice that you experience emotional outbursts less often and that they are not as intense.

- **Decreased instances of self-harm and other impulsive, risky behaviors:** As you recover, you may find that you engage in self-harm or other impulsive, risky behaviors less often.

- **Increased ability to cope with crisis periods:** Even if you still experience occasional setbacks, you may find that you are better able to cope with crisis periods than you were before starting treatment.

- **Increased confidence in your ability to lead a fulfilling and successful life:** As your symptoms improve, you may find that you feel more confident in your ability to live a fulfilling and successful life.

As we come to the end of this chapter, let's review some of the key concepts we've discussed:

This chapter discusses Borderline Personality Disorder, the importance of a support system, how to find a suitable mental healthcare professional, and how to enhance your success in overcoming the disorder.

Key Points:

The Importance of a Support System

- A strong support system is essential for people with BPD. This support system can include family, friends, therapists, or other mental health professionals.

- Family and friends can provide emotional support and help people with BPD cope with their symptoms. Therapists and other mental health professionals can provide treatment and help people with BPD develop coping skills.

Finding a Suitable Mental Healthcare Professional

- It is important to find a mental healthcare professional who is experienced in treating BPD. This professional should be someone you feel comfortable talking to and who you can trust.

- When looking for a therapist, it is helpful to ask questions about their experience with BPD, their treatment approach, and their fees. It is also helpful to schedule a consultation so you can get to know them and see if they are a good fit for you.

Enhancing Your Chances of Success

There are a few things you can do to enhance your chances of success in overcoming BPD. These include:

- **Be an active participant in your treatment.** This means being open and honest with your therapist, working hard to follow their recommendations, and being willing to challenge yourself.

- **Educate yourself about BPD.** The more you know about the disorder, the better equipped you will be to manage your symptoms and cope with challenges.

- **Build a strong support network.** Having people

who care about you and understand what you are going through can make a big difference in your recovery.

- **Practice self-care.** This includes things like getting enough sleep, eating healthy foods, exercising regularly, and taking time for relaxation and stress relief.

- **Be patient with yourself.** Recovery from BPD takes time and effort. Don't get discouraged if you don't see results immediately. Just keep working hard and you will eventually reach your goals.

Recovery from BPD is a complex process. It is marked by decreased frequency and intensity of emotional outbursts, fewer instances of self-harm, an increased ability to cope with crisis periods, and increased confidence in leading a fulfilling life.

We've learned that a strong support network can play a key role in managing borderline personality disorder. In the next chapter, we'll explore all the resources available to help us manage and overcome this disorder.

CHAPTER 10: SOOTHING THE BODY TO SOOTHE THE MIND

Do you ever feel like you're at the mercy of your emotions?

Borderline personality disorder can make it feel like your emotions are out of control. You might feel like you're constantly overreacting, or that your emotions are dictating your behavior.

It can be frustrating and isolating to feel like you're not in control of your own mind. But there is hope.

With the right treatment, you can learn to manage your emotions and regain a sense of control over your life. One of the most effective ways to manage BPD is to **rewire your brain.** Your brain is constantly changing and adapting. When you practice healthy coping mechanisms, you're creating new neural pathways in your brain. The more you practice these coping mechanisms, the stronger these pathways become. Eventually, they will become your brain's default response to stress and difficult emotions.

Awaken Your Senses

Tapping into your senses can be a powerful way to cope with the emotional ups and downs of borderline personality disorder. Everyone experiences the world differently, so it's important to find what works best for you. What helps you feel grounded and calm one day might not work the next.

Here are a few ideas to get you started:

Visual: Look around you and take in the sights. Notice the colors, shapes, and textures of the world around you. You could also try looking at a painting, photograph, or other piece of art that you find visually appealing. Close your eyes and visualize a calming scene. This could be a beach, a forest, or even your own bedroom. Focus on the details of the scene and allow yourself to feel relaxed and at peace.

Gustatory: Engaging your sense of taste can be a powerful way to cope with difficult emotions. When you're feeling empty, try eating something with a strong, bold flavor, like lemons, hot peppers, or mints. These flavors can help to ground you and bring you back into the present moment. Conversely, if you're feeling angry or restless, try eating something warm and soothing, like tea or soup. These foods can help to calm you down and relax your body.

Tactile: When you're feeling numb or overwhelmed, try using your sense of touch to ground yourself. Hold a piece of ice or let warm or cold water run across your hands. The physical sensation can help to bring you back into the present moment. If you're feeling restless or anxious, try squeezing a stress ball or taking a deep-tissue massage. These activities can help to release tension and promote relaxation.

Olfactory: The sense of smell is closely linked to our emotions. Certain scents can have a powerful effect on our mood. For example, the smell of lavender is often associated with relaxation, while the smell of citrus can be energizing. Experiment with different scents to see which ones have a positive effect on your mood. You can try using essential oils, scented candles, or even fresh flowers.

Auditory: The sound of music can also have a powerful effect on our emotions. Listening to calming music can help to reduce stress and anxiety, while listening to upbeat music can help to boost mood. Experiment with different types of music to find what works best for you. You can also try listening to nature sounds, like the waves crashing on the shore or the birds singing in the trees.

Remember, everyone experiences emotions differently. What works for one person may not work for another. The most important thing is to find what works for you and to be patient with yourself. With time and practice, you can learn to use your senses to help you cope with difficult emotions and live a more balanced life.

Soothing Activities for Emotional Regulation

This chapter explored various therapeutic approaches for managing borderline personality disorder, including the importance of psychoeducation, the potential role of medication, and practical self-help strategies.

Key Points:

- **The debilitating impact of BPD:** BPD can have a debilitating impact on a person's emotional control, making it difficult to manage their emotions and maintain healthy relationships.

- **The promise of effective treatments:** There are effective treatments available for BPD that can help people regain a sense of control over their lives.

- **The importance of rewiring the brain:** BPD can change the way the brain functions, but it is possible to rewire the brain using healthy coping mechanisms to create new neural pathways and manage BPD.

- **The power of the senses:** The senses can be a powerful tool for coping with emotional fluctuations associated with BPD. Engaging in activities that stimulate the senses can help to regulate emotions and reduce stress.

Soothing activities for emotional regulation: There are many soothing activities that can be helpful for managing different emotional states, such as anxiety, anger, depression, and loneliness. Some examples include:

- **Taking deep breaths:** Deep breathing can help to calm the body and mind.

- **Practicing mindfulness:** Mindfulness involves focusing on the present moment and accepting thoughts and feelings without judgment.

- **Engaging in physical activity:** Physical activity can help to release endorphins, which have mood-boosting effects.

- **Listening to music:** Listening to calming or upbeat music can help to regulate emotions.

- **Spending time in nature:** Spending time in nature can help to reduce stress and improve mood.

- **The concept of resilience:** Resilience is the ability to bounce back from difficult experiences. It can be cultivated by practicing self-care, building strong relationships, and maintaining a positive outlook.

- **Psychoeducation:** Psychoeducation is a valuable tool for increasing understanding of BPD, exploring treatment options, developing coping strategies, and building support networks. It can be delivered in a variety of formats, such as individual or group sessions, online courses, or workshops.

- **The potential role of medication:** Medication can be a helpful part of treatment for BPD, but it is not a cure. Medication can help to reduce symptoms, such as mood swings, self-harm, and impulsivity. It is important to work with a healthcare professional to find the right medication and dosage.

- **The need for a holistic approach:** BPD is a complex disorder that requires a holistic approach to treatment. This includes psychoeducation, medication, and self-help strategies.

- **The importance of consulting healthcare professionals:** If you are struggling with BPD, it is important to consult healthcare professionals. They can help you to develop a treatment plan that is right for you.

I'm glad you found this chapter helpful! I'm excited to continue our discussion of BPD in the next chapter, where we'll explore specific therapies that can be helpful in managing the disorder. Specifically, we'll discuss cognitive behavioral therapy (CBT) and dialectical behavioral therapy (DBT). CBT is a type of therapy that focuses on changing the way people think and behave. DBT is a type of therapy that combines CBT with mindfulness and acceptance strategies. Both CBT and DBT have been shown to be effective in treating BPD.

CHAPTER 11: MANAGING BORDERLINE PERSONALITY DISORDER WITH COGNITIVE BEHAVIORAL THERAPY AND DIALECTICAL BEHAVIOR THERAPY

Did you know that cognitive behavioral therapy (CBT) and dialectical behavior therapy (DBT) are two types of psychotherapy that have been successfully applied in treating borderline personality disorder?

CBT is a type of therapy that focuses on changing the way people think about and react to their emotions. DBT is a modified form of CBT that also focuses on helping people develop skills to cope with difficult emotions and situations.

Both CBT and DBT have been shown to be effective in treating BPD. In fact, DBT is the only empirically supported treatment for BPD. This means that there is scientific evidence to support its effectiveness.

Cognitive Behavioral Therapy

Cognitive behavioral therapy is a type of therapy that helps people change the way they think and behave. It is based on the idea that our thoughts, feelings, and behaviors are all interconnected. When we have negative thoughts, it can lead to negative feelings and behaviors. CBT can help us to identify and change these negative thoughts, which can lead to positive changes in our feelings and behaviors.

CBT is a short-term, goal-oriented therapy. It is commonly used to treat a range of disorders including depression, anxiety, addictions, and phobias. CBT is often more affordable than other types of therapies because it is typically a shorter-term treatment. CBT usually focuses on helping clients deal with a very specific problem.

How CBT Works

CBT works on the premise that our behavior is heavily influenced by our thoughts and feelings. For example, someone with low self-esteem may believe that when they are in public, people are constantly judging them. As a result, they shy away from social occasions and prefer to spend time alone. CBT aims to teach patients that they cannot control every element in the world around them, but they are responsible for the way they perceive these external events.

One of the main goals of CBT is to help patients identify and change their negative thoughts. These negative thoughts, often called "automatic thoughts," can be things like "I'm not good enough" or "I'll never succeed." Automatic thoughts often have their roots in early childhood experiences and can pop into our heads without us having any control over them. When we believe these negative thoughts, they can have a significant impact on our mood and can contribute to depression, anxiety, and other emotional difficulties.

The first step in CBT is to identify the automatic thoughts that are causing problems for the client. The therapist will work with the client to identify these thoughts and to understand how they are affecting the client's behavior. This can be a challenging process, especially for someone who is not used to introspection.

The second step in CBT is to challenge these negative thoughts. The therapist will help the client to gather evidence to support or refute these thoughts. For example, the client who believes that people are always judging them might be asked to think about a time when they felt this way and to consider whether there is any evidence to support this belief.

Once the client has challenged their negative thoughts, they can begin to develop more positive and realistic thoughts. The therapist will help the client to develop these new thoughts and to practice using them in their everyday life.

CBT is a collaborative therapy, which means that the therapist and the client work together to create a treatment plan that is tailored to the client's individual needs. CBT is a short-term, goal-oriented therapy that can be an effective treatment for a variety of mental health problems. If you are struggling with a mental health problem, CBT may be a helpful option for you.

Here are some additional things to keep in mind about CBT:

- CBT is a collaborative therapy, which means that the therapist and the client work together to create a treatment plan that is tailored to the client's individual needs.

- CBT is a short-term therapy, which means that it typically lasts for 12-16 weeks.

- CBT is a goal-oriented therapy, which means that the therapist and the client work together to set specific goals for therapy.

- CBT is a structured therapy, which means that the therapist uses a specific set of techniques to help the client change their thinking and behavior.

- CBT is a research-supported therapy, which means that there is a lot of evidence to support its effectiveness.

Dialectical Behavioral Therapy

Dialectical behavioral therapy is a type of psychotherapy that focuses on helping people accept their emotions and situations while also working towards positive change. DBT was originally developed to treat borderline personality disorder, but it has since been shown to be effective in treating a variety of other mental health conditions, including depression, anxiety, substance abuse, and eating disorders.

DBT is a skills-based therapy that teaches people four key skills:

- **Mindfulness:** This skill involves learning to pay attention to the present moment without judgment. Mindfulness can help people to become more aware of their thoughts, feelings, and bodily sensations, which can help them to better understand and manage their emotions.

- **Distress tolerance:** This skill helps people to cope with difficult emotions and situations in a healthy way. Distress tolerance skills can help people to avoid self-destructive behaviors, such as substance abuse or self-harm, and to cope with difficult emotions in a more constructive way.

- **Interpersonal effectiveness:** This skill helps people to communicate their needs and wants in a clear and assertive way. Interpersonal effectiveness skills can help people to build healthier relationships and to resolve conflicts in a more constructive way.

- **Emotional regulation:** This skill helps people to manage their emotions in a healthy way. Emotional regulation skills can help people to identify their emotions, to understand the triggers that cause them to experience these emotions, and to develop healthy coping mechanisms for dealing with these emotions.

DBT is typically delivered through a combination of individual therapy, group therapy, and phone coaching. The structure of DBT ensures that the therapeutic strategies are not just theoretical but are practiced and reinforced in the patient's daily life.

DBT is a compassionate and effective treatment that can help people to live more fulfilling and meaningful lives. If you are struggling with a mental health condition, I encourage you to talk to your doctor or a mental health professional about whether DBT may be a helpful option for you.

Here are some additional things to keep in mind about DBT:

- DBT is a long-term treatment. It typically takes 12-18 months to complete.

- DBT is a skills-based treatment. This means that you will learn skills that you can use to manage your emotions and to live a more fulfilling life.

- DBT is a collaborative treatment. This means that you will work with your therapist to develop a treatment plan that is tailored to your individual needs.

- DBT is a supportive treatment. Your therapist will provide you with support and encouragement as you work through the program.

We have reached the end of this chapter, so let's take a moment to review the key points:

We have explored two significant types of psychotherapy, cognitive behavioral therapy and dialectical behavior therapy, and their applications, strategies, and impact in treating mental health disorders such as borderline personality disorder. CBT and DBT are two forms of psychotherapy that can be helpful for people with BPD and other mental health conditions.

Key Points:

- **CBT:** CBT helps people change the way they think about and react to their emotions. It is based on the idea that our thoughts, feelings, and behaviors are all interconnected. When we have negative thoughts, it can lead to negative feelings and behaviors. CBT can help people identify and change these negative thoughts, which can lead to positive changes in their feelings and behaviors.

- **DBT:** DBT is a modified form of CBT that also focuses on helping people develop skills to cope with difficult emotions and situations. DBT is especially helpful for people with BPD, who often experience intense emotions and have difficulty coping with them. DBT teaches four main skills: mindfulness, distress tolerance, interpersonal effectiveness, and emotional regulation.

Both CBT and DBT are collaborative therapies, which means that the therapist and the client work together to create a treatment plan that is tailored to the client's individual needs. Both therapies are also short-term, goal-oriented therapies, which means that they are designed to help people achieve specific goals in a relatively short period of time.

That's all for now. In the next chapter, we will explore other effective ways to manage borderline personality disorder.

CHAPTER 12: OTHER EFFECTIVE TREATMENTS FOR BPD

The journey of understanding and managing Borderline Personality Disorder can be challenging, but there are many different therapeutic approaches that can help. These methods offer a wealth of strategies and exercises that can help individuals with BPD regain control over their thoughts, feelings, and behaviors.

This chapter will explore three such approaches: Mentalization-Based Therapy (MBT), Transference-Focused Psychotherapy (TFP), and Schema-Focused Therapy (SFT). These therapies are all evidence-based and have been shown to be effective in treating BPD.

Mentalization-Based Therapy (MBT)

Mentalization-Based Therapy (MBT) is a therapeutic approach that helps people understand their own mental states and the mental states of others. MBT was developed by Peter Fonagy and Anthony Bateman, and it aims to improve a person's capacity for mentalization, which is the ability to understand behavior in terms of thoughts, feelings, desires, and beliefs, both in oneself and others.

Practical Example

Let's imagine a person with BPD named Alex. Alex often reacts impulsively to situations, which leads to frequent conflicts with people around him. During a session of MBT, Alex expresses that he recently got into an argument with his colleague at work because he felt his colleague was ignoring him.

The therapist might guide Alex through the process of mentalization by asking him to think about what he was feeling at the moment when he believed his colleague was ignoring him. Alex might realize that he was feeling neglected or dismissed.

The therapist might then encourage Alex to reflect on what thoughts or beliefs could have led to those feelings. Alex might then realize that he had interpreted his colleague's silence as a personal slight, which may not necessarily have been the case.

The therapist would then guide Alex to consider other potential reasons for his colleague's behavior. Perhaps his colleague was preoccupied with their own concerns or deadlines and did not intend to ignore Alex.

By understanding his own feelings and considering the potential thoughts and feelings of his colleague, Alex can start to react less impulsively and improve his interactions with others.

MBT offers a unique approach to psychotherapy that can lead to a more grounded and compassionate self-view, as well as improved interpersonal relationships. It is important to note that while MBT can be particularly beneficial for individuals with BPD, its effectiveness can be enhanced when combined with other therapeutic methods.

Like any therapy, the success of MBT greatly depends on the therapeutic alliance and the individual's willingness to engage with the process. It is also important to remember that the process can be challenging, and patience and consistent effort are key.

MBT is a complex and challenging therapy, but it can be a valuable tool for people with BPD and other mental health conditions. If you are considering MBT, it is important to find a trained mental health professional who can help you assess whether it is the right therapy for you.

Transference-Focused Psychotherapy (TFP)

Transference-Focused Psychotherapy (TFP) is a type of psychotherapy that is specifically designed to help individuals with Borderline Personality Disorder (BPD). TFP is a psychodynamic therapy that focuses on the dynamics that develop in the relationship between the therapist and the patient. The idea is that the individual with BPD will inevitably begin to view and interact with the therapist in ways that mirror their other relationships. This "transference" of feelings, behaviors, and perceptions from past relationships onto the therapist offers a valuable window into how the individual interacts with others. By understanding and working through these dynamics in the therapy session, the patient can gain insights into their emotions and interpersonal difficulties and apply this understanding to other relationships in their life.

TFP is an intensive, long-term therapy that requires commitment from both the therapist and the patient. It can lead to profound changes in self-perception and relationships. **The process of TFP typically involves the following steps:**

1. **Building the therapeutic alliance:** The therapist establishes a supportive, non-judgmental relationship with the patient. The patient should feel understood

and accepted, which encourages them to open up about their thoughts and emotions.

2. **Observing transference:** As the therapy progresses, patterns will begin to emerge in how the patient relates to the therapist. For instance, the patient might start viewing the therapist as a neglectful parent or a dismissive friend. These patterns are not consciously chosen by the patient; they are the "transferences" from their past relationships.

3. **Interpreting transference:** The therapist gently points out these patterns to the patient, framing them as hypotheses rather than facts. For instance, the therapist might say, "I noticed you seemed angry when I didn't return your call immediately. It made me wonder if you were feeling neglected or abandoned, like you sometimes felt in your relationship with your parents."

4. **Examining and gaining insight:** Together, the therapist and the patient explore these patterns, their origins, and how they might be influencing the patient's current relationships and self-perception. This examination fosters a deeper understanding of their emotions and interpersonal difficulties.

5. **Applying insights to the patient's life:** The patient applies this understanding to their relationships outside therapy. They might start recognizing when they are projecting past relationship dynamics onto present ones, and choose to react differently.

TFP is an effective therapy for BPD, but it is not without its challenges. The process can be emotionally challenging, as it involves confronting and working through painful experiences and feelings. It requires patience, persistence, and the willingness to engage deeply with one's emotional world. The success of TFP largely depends on the therapeutic relationship and the patient's readiness and capacity to engage in introspective work. It's therefore crucial that this approach is carried out by a trained professional who can provide a safe, supportive space for this process to unfold.

Schema-Focused Therapy (SFT)

Schema-Focused Therapy (SFT) is a therapeutic approach that integrates elements of cognitive behavioral therapy (CBT), psychoanalytic object relations therapy, and the techniques of gestalt therapy. It was specifically developed to treat personality disorders such as borderline personality disorder (BPD).

SFT aims to change the way individuals perceive themselves by identifying and addressing lifelong, self-defeating patterns, known as "schemas." Schemas are deep-seated and enduring patterns in thinking and behavior that can often lead to self-destructive actions or problematic interpersonal relationships. By addressing these schemas, the individual can start to replace them with healthier ways of thinking, feeling, and behaving.

The process of SFT typically involves the following steps:

1. **Schema assessment:** The therapist and the patient work together to identify the individual's schemas. They will typically use questionnaires, interviews, or other assessment tools. The therapist might ask about the patient's childhood experiences, current relationships, and recurring patterns in their life.

2. **Emotional awareness and expression:** The therapist helps the patient to become aware of the emotions connected to their schemas and to express these emotions in a safe environment. This might involve techniques from gestalt therapy, such as role-playing or two-chair exercises.

3. **Cognitive restructuring:** The therapist helps the patient to challenge their schemas by examining the evidence for and against them. The patient learns to recognize when their schemas are activated, and to replace their habitual reactions with healthier responses.

4. **Behavioral change:** The patient puts their new ways of thinking into practice in their everyday life. They might confront situations they used to avoid or respond differently to situations that used to trigger their schemas. The therapist provides support and guidance throughout this process.

5. **Maintenance:** As the patient begins to experience improvements in their life, the therapist helps them to consolidate their new, healthier patterns of thinking, feeling, and behaving. The patient learns to anticipate potential challenges and to use their new skills to navigate these challenges effectively.

SFT is a long-term therapeutic approach that requires commitment and active participation from the patient. It can be intense and challenging at times, as it involves revisiting past traumas and confronting deeply ingrained patterns. However, the rewards can be profound, including improved self-esteem, healthier relationships, and greater life satisfaction. The therapy should always be conducted by a trained professional to ensure the patient's safety and well-being. Lastly, it's important to remember that progress may be slow and non-linear, and patience is required. It's crucial not to rush the process and to give oneself the necessary time and space for healing to occur.

Did you find these other techniques for managing borderline personality disorder helpful? Before we move on to the next chapter, let's take a moment to summarize what we learned.

In this chapter, we explored three therapeutic approaches that can be helpful for managing BPD: mentalization-based therapy (MBT), transference-focused psychotherapy (TFP), and schema-focused therapy (SFT).

Key Points:

- **MBT** helps people with BPD to understand their own and others' mental states and emotions. This can be helpful for people with BPD who often have difficulty understanding their own emotions and why they behave the way they do. MBT also helps people with BPD to develop better coping skills and to improve their relationships.

- **TFP** focuses on the relationship between the therapist and the patient. This approach helps people with BPD to understand how their past relationships have shaped their current thoughts, feelings, and behaviors. TFP can also help people with BPD to develop healthier ways of relating to others.

- **SFT** is an integrated therapeutic approach that focuses on identifying and addressing self-defeating patterns or schemas. Schemas are core beliefs that people develop in childhood about themselves and the world around them. These beliefs can be negative and harmful, and they can lead to problems in relationships, work, and other areas of life. SFT can help people with BPD to identify their schemas and to develop healthier ways of thinking and behaving.

All three of these approaches can be helpful for managing BPD, but they are not right for everyone. It is important to work with a therapist who is experienced in treating BPD and who can help you to determine which approach is right for you.

I hope the examples of these exercises have helped you understand the many ways you can manage your condition. In the next part of the book, we'll focus on those who live with you every day and love you. With a few helpful tips, they can stand by you and help you in the best way possible.

PART 2: STRATEGIES FOR HELPING A LOVED ONE WITH BORDERLINE PERSONALITY DISORDER

CHAPTER 13: EDUCATING YOURSELF AND YOUR FAMILY ABOUT BPD

Do you feel like you're constantly struggling with Borderline Personality Disorder? Do you feel like the challenges of BPD are insurmountable, especially in your relationships?

Welcome to the second part of this book, which is dedicated to those who want to help a loved one with BPD. It can be challenging to live with borderline personality disorder, but it is also challenging to be a loved one of someone with BPD. We all crave connection and understanding from the people around us. But if you have BPD, it can feel like you're walking on a tightrope, desperately trying to balance. The world can seem like an overwhelming sea of judgment and misunderstanding, and you might feel like retreating into isolation. You might look back at a past marred with severed relationships and hurt, and feel like hope is slipping away. It can feel like you're adrift in a dark ocean, longing for the world to forget you exist.

But there is hope. Amidst all of this struggle, there is a silver lining. Your salvation lies in building a strong support network. These connections will be your beacon, guiding you through the stormy waters of BPD. The stronger your support network, the brighter your chances of mastering the turmoil and embracing a fulfilling life. Yes, it's challenging, but isn't the promise of such a life worth the fight?

How to Help Your Loved One Navigate BPD: Insights for Families

Borderline Personality Disordercan be a challenging disorder for both the person with BPD and their loved ones. It can be difficult to understand and cope with, and it can often lead to conflict and tension. However, there are things that families can do to help their loved ones with BPD.

One of the most important things is to **educate yourself about BPD**. This means learning about the symptoms, the causes, and the treatment options. There are many resources available to help families learn about BPD, including books, websites, and support groups.

Once you understand BPD, you can start to **offer support to your loved one**. This support can take many forms, such as listening to them, offering encouragement, and helping them to find treatment. It is also important to be **patient and understanding**, as BPD can be a challenging disorder.

Finally, you may want to consider **participating in family psychoeducation sessions**. These sessions are led by a therapist and provide families with information about BPD, as well as strategies for coping with the disorder. By taking these steps, you can help your loved one with BPD to live a more fulfilling life.

Here are some specific tips for families of people with BPD:

- **Talk to your loved one about their diagnosis**. This will help you to understand what they are going through and how you can best support them.

- **Ask your loved one's therapist for information about BPD**. This will help you to learn more about the disorder and how it affects your loved one.

- **Offer your loved one unconditional love and sup-**

port. This is essential for their well-being.

- **Be patient and understanding**. BPD can be a challenging disorder, so it is important to be patient with your loved one.

- **Set boundaries**. It is important to set boundaries with your loved one, especially if their behavior is harmful to you or others.

- **Seek professional help**. If you are struggling to cope with your loved one's BPD, seek professional help. A therapist can help you to develop coping strategies and support you through this difficult time.

Navigating Love & BPD: A Guide for Partners

If you're living with borderline personality disorder, you know how difficult it can be to navigate romantic relationships. The fear of rejection and emotional instability that comes with BPD can often lead to a series of dramatic relationships.

But BPD doesn't have to be a barrier to a fulfilling relationship. Many people with BPD maintain loving, supportive relationships, with understanding and communication being the key ingredients to success.

One of the most important things you can do to help your partner understand your experiences is to **share your perspective**. Let them know how your fear of rejection and abandonment can trigger negative emotions and distress, even when there is no real threat. Help them understand how your anger can sneak up unexpectedly, and that your heightened reactions are a product of BPD, not a response to their actions or inactions.

It's also important to **discuss your BPD symptoms** with your partner. Explain how BPD amplifies both positive and negative emotions, and how you often find it challenging to interpret facial expressions alone. Share your tendency towards dichotomous thinking, and how you can swing between seeing things as all good or all bad.

Being in a relationship with someone with BPD can be challenging, but it's important to remember that you're not alone. There are many resources available to help you and your partner navigate BPD together.

Here are some strategies that can help you manage BPD effectively in your relationship:

- **Ensure conversations happen when both parties are calm.** BPD episodes can trigger strong emotional reactions in your partner. Discuss important matters only when both of you are calm and composed.

- **Empower your partner with knowledge about BPD.** Understanding your daily struggles can enhance empathy and acceptance that your challenging behavior is due to an illness, not personal choice.

- **Consider professional help.** Engaging a mental health professional can be beneficial for both of you, either individually or as a couple.

- **Prioritize communication.** When BPD is part of the relationship, effective communication is paramount. Always approach conversations with love and understanding that what may seem like hurtful behavior may just be your partner trying to navigate the situation.

- **Encourage your partner not to attribute everything to your mental illness.** Help them realize that you are more than your BPD, and labeling everything as such can be disheartening.

- **Promote your partner's self-care.** Living with a partner with BPD can be demanding. It's crucial to recognize their struggles and ensure they have their own support network and self-care rituals. Allow them to have their own space, hobbies, and social interactions, understanding that as much as they support you, they too need a balanced life.

Navigating BPD in a relationship can be challenging, but it's also an opportunity to grow closer and build a stronger foundation for your relationship. With understanding, communication, and support, you can overcome any obstacle that comes your way.

Helping Your Children Understand BPD: A Parent's Guide

Parenting is a demanding role, even under the best circumstances. But when you have borderline personality disorder, it can be even more challenging. BPD can make it difficult to be consistent and can leave you feeling ill-equipped as a parent.

Unfortunately, many children of parents with BPD may later struggle with attachment issues and other complications in their adulthood. This underscores the importance of seeking comprehensive support when raising children with BPD.

Navigating parenthood with BPD is a journey best undertaken alongside your therapist or doctor. However, here are a few strategies that could help:

- **Consider enlisting a professional family support service to visit your home and interact with your child.** This can give you some much-needed respite and time for self-care, and it can also help your child to better understand your condition.

- **Participate in individual therapy sessions to manage your emotions, specifically those associated with parenthood and fears regarding your child's upbringing.** This can help you to develop healthier coping mechanisms and to better understand your child's needs.

- **Engage in group therapy sessions with your child to bolster your relationship.** These sessions can be vital in mitigating potential attachment issues in your children, and they can also help your child to feel more connected to you.

- **Arrange occasional caregiving for your child by someone else, either in childcare or by a trusted family member.** This will give you a necessary break and allow you to focus on your own mental health.

- **Similar to managing relationships with adults, it can be beneficial for your children to understand your condition.** Use age-appropriate books and stories to explain your illness and its implications. Incorporating discussions about mental health and well-being can help them better understand your erratic behavior, and also encourage them to open up about their own feelings and difficulties. Consultation with a child psychologist could be highly beneficial in this context.

- **If you have an infant and need to be hospitalized, try to keep your baby with you during this period.** This will help to minimize the disruption to your child's routine and to maintain your bond with them.

Ultimately, the most beneficial thing you can do for your children is to commit to your treatment, striving towards better mental health while minimizing their exposure to the more challenging aspects of BPD.

I know that parenting with BPD can be a daunting task, but it is important to remember that you are not alone. There are many resources available to help you, and you can do this.

Before we turn the page, let's take a moment to review the key takeaways from this chapter. This will help us to solidify our understanding of the material and to ensure that we are on the same page:

This chapter provides strategies for managing borderline personality disorder within various types of relationships, such as those with family, romantic partners, and children.

Key Points:

- **The importance of a strong support network.** Having a strong support network can be invaluable for those struggling with BPD. This network can provide you with love, support, and understanding when you need it most.

- **The importance of educating yourself and your family about BPD.** The more you know about BPD, the better equipped you will be to support your loved one. There are many resources available to help you learn about BPD, such as books, websites, and support groups.

- **Effective communication and setting boundaries.** Communication is key in any relationship, but it is especially important in relationships with someone who has BPD. It is important to be able to communicate your needs and boundaries in a clear and respectful way.

- **The significance of professional help and family psychoeducation sessions.** Professional help can be a valuable resource for those struggling with BPD. A therapist can help you develop coping mechanisms and strategies for managing your symptoms. Family psychoeducation sessions can also be helpful for educating your family about BPD and how to best support you.

- **The unique challenges and strategies associated with romantic relationships involving a partner with BPD.** Romantic relationships can be especially challenging for those with BPD. It is important to be open and honest with your partner about your condition, and to seek professional help if you are struggling.

- **The necessity for open communication, understanding, and professional assistance in these relationships.** Open communication, understanding, and professional assistance are essential for maintaining healthy and fulfilling romantic relationships involving someone with BPD.

- **How to navigate the complexities of parenting when suffering from BPD.** Parenting can be a complex and challenging task for anyone, but it can be especially challenging for those with BPD. It is important to seek professional help if you are struggling to parent effectively.

- **Suggestions on seeking professional help, communicating the condition to children, and maintaining self-care and mental health stability.** There are many resources available to help parents with BPD. It is important to seek professional help, communicate the condition to your children in an age-appropriate way, and maintain your own self-care and mental health stability.

- **The emphasis on commitment to treatment for the benefit of both oneself and one's children.** Commitment to treatment is essential for both the individual with BPD and their children. With treatment, it is possible to manage BPD and maintain healthy and fulfilling relationships.

Our journey is not over yet. In the following pages, we will discuss the challenges of starting a relationship with someone with borderline personality disorder.

CHAPTER 14: THE CHALLENGES AND REWARDS OF BEING IN A RELATIONSHIP WITH SOMEONE WITH BORDERLINE PERSONALITY DISORDER

Are you drawn to charismatic and energetic individuals?

Many people are drawn to the captivating allure of people with borderline personality disorder. These individuals are often charming, exciting, and passionate. However, their unique challenges can lead to a cycle of recurring disagreements and intense situations, which can be taxing for their partners.

Does this mean that you should avoid relationships with people who have BPD?

Not necessarily. If you deeply care for and love your partner, such a relationship may still hold immense worth. However, it is important to understand what to expect and how your partner's disorder may manifest itself. With understanding and support, you can build a fulfilling and meaningful bond with your partner.

Getting Into Your Partner's Mind

Understanding borderline personality disorder is essential for understanding the emotional whirlwind that your partner may be experiencing. In Part One of this book, you can learn more about BPD, its origins, and its various manifestations. However, some BPD traits often take center stage in romantic relationships.

People with BPD **often experience intense emotions, both positive and negative.** They may feel joy, gratitude, and love intensely, but they may also feel anger, sadness, and fear intensely. This emotional intensity can be overwhelming for both the person with BPD and their partner.

People with BPD often have a **fear of abandonment.** This fear can be triggered by even the slightest perceived threat of rejection or loss. As a result, people with BPD may become clingy or demanding, or they may push their partners away in an attempt to avoid being hurt.

People with BPD often engage in **black-and-white thinking**, which means that they see things in terms of extremes. This can lead them to view their partners as either all good or all bad. When their partners do something that they perceive as negative, they may suddenly switch from feeling love and admiration to feeling disappointment and disdain.

It is important to remember that these are just some of the BPD traits that can manifest in romantic relationships. Everyone with BPD is different, and their experiences will vary. However, understanding these traits can help you to better understand your partner and their behavior.

Navigating the Waves

Being in a relationship with someone who has borderline personality disorder can be a rollercoaster ride. You may feel like you are giving your all, but it may not seem like your partner is reciprocating. The turmoil and confusion can be overwhelming, and you may start to question your own ability to sustain the relationship.

If you are feeling this way, you are not alone. Many people who are in relationships with people with BPD experience these same feelings. However, there are things you can do to make life with a BPD partner more manageable.

Here are some tips:

- **Educate yourself about BPD.** The more you know about the disorder, the more understanding you will be of your partner's behavior. You will also be better able to cope with the challenges that come with being in a relationship with someone with BPD.

- **Seek professional help.** Therapy can be a great way to learn more about BPD and to develop coping mechanisms for dealing with the challenges of the disorder. You may also want to consider couples therapy to help you and your partner communicate more effectively.

- **Prioritize communication.** Communication is key in any relationship, but it is especially important in relationships with people with BPD. Be clear and direct in your communication, and avoid making assumptions or jumping to conclusions. When you communicate with your partner, be mindful of their emotional state and try to be as supportive as possible.

- **Be supportive.** Let your partner know that you are

there for them, no matter what. Offer your support during both good times and bad. This could mean providing emotional support, practical help, or simply being a listening ear.

- **Encourage independence.** It is important for people with BPD to have a sense of independence. Encourage your partner to have their own interests and hobbies, and to spend time with their own friends. This will help them to feel more grounded and less reliant on you for their emotional needs.

- **Avoid labeling.** BPD is just one aspect of your partner's identity. Avoid labeling them as "BPD" or "crazy." See them as the unique and complex individual that they are.

- **Take self-harm threats seriously.** If your partner threatens self-harm or suicide, take it seriously. Do not dismiss their threats or try to downplay them. Get help immediately. This could mean calling 911 or taking your partner to the emergency room.

- **Prioritize self-care.** It is important to take care of yourself, both physically and emotionally. Make sure you are getting enough sleep, eating healthy foods, and exercising regularly. You should also have a support network of friends and family who can offer you support during difficult times.

Navigating the waves of a relationship with someone with BPD can be challenging, but it is possible to have a fulfilling and loving relationship. By following these tips, you can learn to cope with the challenges of BPD and build a strong and healthy relationship with your partner.

Are you interested in learning how to communicate effectively with someone who has borderline personality disorder? If so, I invite you to join me in the next chapter.

CHAPTER 15: HOW TO COMMUNICATE EFFECTIVELY WITH SOMEONE WHO HAS BORDERLINE PERSONALITY DISORDER

What does the heart of a person with Borderline Personality Disorder yearn for?

People with BPD often feel like they are on the outside looking in. They may feel like they don't belong anywhere and that no one truly understands them. They may also feel like they are constantly being judged and criticized.

What do they really want?

Deep down, people with BPD just want to be loved and accepted for who they are. They want to feel like they belong and that they are not alone. They want to feel like they are worthy of love and happiness.

What makes it difficult for them to feel loved?

BPD can make it difficult for people to feel loved. Their emotional sensitivity can make them feel like even the smallest criticism is a personal attack. They may also misinterpret conversations, feeling hurt where no insult was intended.

How can you communicate with someone with BPD in an empathetic way?

Here are a few ways to speak to and relate to a friend, partner, or family member who is suffering from borderline personality disorder:

- **Strive for clarity in your communication:** Be clear and direct in your communication, and avoid relying on subtle cues or facial expressions to convey your message. This can help to reduce misunderstandings and conflict.

- **Be consistently supportive:** Be there for your loved one, both emotionally and practically. This means being available to listen, offer help, and provide comfort when needed.

- **Validate their experiences:** Even if you don't understand your loved one's feelings, acknowledge them as valid and real. This can help them to feel understood and supported.

- **Show your understanding:** If you can relate to your loved one's feelings, let them know. If you don't, express a desire to learn more and understand better. This can help to build trust and communication.

- **Offer hope:** Share stories of other BPD sufferers who have found happiness and stability. This can help to give your loved one hope for the future.

- **Acknowledge their struggle:** BPD can be a difficult disorder to live with. Acknowledge your loved one's struggle, and help them to break down goals into smaller, achievable steps. This can help to keep them motivated and on track.

- **Maintain realistic expectations:** BPD can involve many setbacks. Maintain realistic expectations, and remain positive and encouraging. This can help to keep your loved one motivated and hopeful.

- **If appropriate, inquire about their BPD management plan:** Discuss how you can help implement it. This can help to ensure that your loved one is getting the support they need.

- **Clearly communicate your boundaries:** Make sure your loved one understands what behavior you will not tolerate, such as abusive language, violence, or threats. This can help to protect yourself and your relationship.

- **If they become agitated, respond calmly:** If you feel unsafe, leave the situation and seek help. Remaining calm can help to de-escalate the situation and prevent further conflict.

- **Practice active listening and reflection:** Even if you disagree with your loved one, understand that listening doesn't equate to agreeing. This can help to build trust and communication.

- **Encourage open dialogue:** Ask questions like "What happened today that made you feel this way?" or "How has your week been?" This can help your loved one feel heard and valued.

- **Summarize what they've shared with you:** This

can help your loved one feel heard and understood.

- **Focus on the emotions behind their words:** BPD may cause your loved one to express themselves in ways that feel hurtful. Try to understand the core emotion beneath and validate it.

Here are some practices to avoid when caring for a loved one with BPD:

- **Don't try to control their life.** Your loved one with BPD is an adult who is capable of making their own decisions. Instead, offer your support and guidance, but let them make their own choices.

- **Don't get drawn into their conflicts with others.** People with BPD may try to manipulate those around them into engaging in their conflicts. If you find yourself getting drawn into a conflict, take a step back and remind yourself that it is not your responsibility to solve their problems.

- **Don't try to dismiss or invalidate their feelings.** People with BPD often have intense emotions, and it is important to validate their feelings, even if you don't understand them. Let them know that you understand how they are feeling and that you are there for them.

- **Don't take on the role of their therapist.** While you can offer your loved one support, you are not a therapist. If they need professional help, encourage them to seek it out.

- **Don't become defensive.** People with BPD may say things that are hurtful or challenging. It is important to remember that this is not about you, but a manifestation of their disorder. Try to stay calm and understanding, and remind yourself that you love this person.

How to Maintain Effective Communication During a Crisis

When a loved one with BPD is experiencing an episode, they may act out aggressively, throw hurtful accusations, or insult you. It can be natural to feel defensive and respond with hostility in these situations. However, it is important to remember that people with BPD often struggle to see things from another's perspective and may not be able to distinguish between minor issues and major crises. If you react defensively, they may interpret this as a sign of abandonment, which can trigger their fears and lead to reckless or self-harming behavior.

Instead, when your loved one becomes reactive, try to listen to them with empathy. This means truly listening to what they are saying, without necessarily agreeing with them or contesting their argument. It is also important to try not to **take their attacks personally.** Remember that their behavior is often a reflection of their pain and confusion, not a reflection of you.

If your loved one points out something you did wrong or an area where you could improve, acknowledge their viewpoint and apologize sincerely. This shows that you are taking them seriously and that you are willing to work on the relationship. When someone with BPD feels heard and taken seriously, it often de-escalates the situation and reduces the chance of it spiraling out of control.

However, if the conflict escalates to threats, aggression, or un-controllable outbursts, it is advisable to remove yourself from the situation and resume the conversation when they have calmed down. This is a safer and more productive way to handle heightened emotional states during a BPD episode.

Recognizing Emergencies and Navigating Through Them

People with borderline personality disorder often struggle with intense emotions, and this can sometimes lead to self-harm or suicidal thoughts. It is important to be aware of the signs of a crisis, so that you can get help if needed.

Some subtle signs that someone may be considering self-harm or suicide include:

- **Sudden changes in behavior**, such as withdrawing from others, losing interest in activities they used to enjoy, or giving away possessions.

- **Changes in mood**, such as becoming more depressed, anxious, or irritable.

- **Changes in thinking**, such as having thoughts of worthlessness or hopelessness.

- **Changes in behavior**, such as engaging in risky or impulsive activities.

If you notice any of these signs, it is important to talk to the person about your concerns. Let them know that you are there for them and that you want to help. You can also offer to help them find professional help.

If you are concerned that the person is in immediate danger of harming themselves or others, call 911 or your local emergency number. You can also call a suicide prevention hotline, such as the National Suicide Prevention Lifeline at 1-800-273-8255.

It is important to remember that you are not alone. There are many people who care about you and want to help. If you are struggling to cope with a loved one's BPD, there are also resources available to help you. You can find more information on the National Alliance on Mental Illness (NAMI) website at https://www.nami.org/.

Here are some tips for navigating a crisis with a loved one with BPD:

- **Stay calm and be supportive.** It can be difficult to stay calm when someone you love is in crisis, but it is important to do so. Your loved one needs your support, and they will be more likely to listen to you if you are calm.

- **Listen to your loved one.** Let them know that you are there for them and that you want to listen to what they have to say. Don't try to solve their problems for them, just listen and offer your support.

- **Avoid arguing or getting defensive.** It is important to avoid arguing with your loved one or getting defensive. This will only make the situation worse.

- **Encourage professional help.** If your loved one is in crisis, encourage them to seek professional help. There are many effective treatments available for BPD, and professional help can make a big difference.

Handling Personal Overwhelm

It is understandable that caring for a loved one with border-line personality disorder can be overwhelming. You may feel exhausted, stressed, and unsure about your ability to cope. It is important to remember that you are not alone and that there are resources available to help you.

One of the best things you can do for yourself is to establish a strong support network. This could include friends, family, therapists, or other healthcare professionals who understand BPD. Having people to talk to and lean on during difficult times can make a big difference.

It is also important to take care of yourself. Make sure you are getting enough sleep, eating healthy foods, and exercising regularly. These activities can help you manage stress and improve your overall well-being.

If you are feeling overwhelmed, it is okay to ask for help. There are many resources available, such as support groups, online forums, and hotlines. You can also talk to your loved one's therapist about how to get the support you need.

Managing Your Expectations Around Recovery

Recovery from BPD is a long and gradual process. There will be ups and downs along the way. It is important to have realistic expectations and to be patient.

Some signs that your loved one is recovering include:

- Less frequent emotional outbursts

- Less intense emotional outbursts

- Decreased instances of self-harm and impulsive behavior

- More rapid resolution of crises

- Increased confidence and motivation

It is important to remember that recovery is not always linear. There may be setbacks along the way. However, with consistent support, your loved one can make progress towards recovery.

Well, this important chapter has also come to an end:

This chapter explored the challenges and rewards of loving and caring for someone with borderline personality disorder. People with BPD often yearn for acceptance, love, and a sense of belonging. However, their intense emotional sensitivity and frequent misinterpretations can make it difficult for them to feel loved.

Key Points:

- **Effective communication:** When dealing with a loved one with BPD, it is important to communicate effectively. This means being clear and direct in your communication, offering support, validating their experiences, and demonstrating understanding. It is also important to be patient and understanding, as people with BPD often have difficulty regulating their emotions.

- **Recognizing emergencies:** If you are concerned that your loved one with BPD is in danger of self-harm or suicide, it is important to recognize the signs of an emergency. These signs may include sudden changes in behavior or mood, thoughts of worthlessness or hopelessness, or threats of self-harm. If you see any of these signs, it is important to seek professional help immediately.

- **Managing personal overwhelm:** Caring for someone with BPD can be challenging, and it is important to manage your own personal overwhelm. This means taking care of yourself, establishing a support network, and seeking help when you need it.

- **Setting realistic expectations:** Recovery from BPD is a gradual process, and it is important to set realistic expectations. There will be ups and downs along the way, but with consistent support, your loved one can make progress towards recovery.

Loving and caring for someone with BPD can be a rewarding experience, but it is important to be aware of the challenges and to seek help when needed. I hope these insights will inspire you to reflect on how you communicate and approach this condition. In the following chapter, we will explore further insights into romantic relationships.

CHAPTER 16: SUPPORTING A PARTNER WITH BORDERLINE PERSONALITY DISORDER

Is your daily life entangled with the seemingly overwhelming challenge of a loved one suffering from Borderline Personality Disorder?

Living with a loved one who has BPD can be incredibly challenging. You may feel like you are on an exhausting roller coaster ride, one filled with moments of terror, aggression, and relentless demands. You may live in a constant state of dread, fearing they might harm themselves if their needs aren't met. Or perhaps you are persistently dealing with their unpredictable behaviors, like erratic requests for money or overwhelming communication. Navigating the complexities of BPD can be daunting, feeling like an unending battle with little reward.

However, with a blend of empathy, understanding, and practical strategies, it is possible to deescalate the crises associated with BPD and foster independence in your loved one. The pathway to their recovery might appear arduous, but it is certainly achievable with the right guidance.

To better manage BPD, it is crucial to understand what your loved one is enduring. An empathetic perspective not only fosters compassion but also equips you to anticipate potential crises and handle them more effectively. So, let's delve into the world of someone living with BPD.

Firstly, it is important to accept BPD as a profound disability that severely limits the quality of life. As you might already observe, it disrupts romantic relationships, friendships, and career prospects, casting a shadow on the individual's overall happiness. Factors like chemical imbalances in the brain and deeply ingrained childhood traumas render life with BPD challenging. Compounded by the potential for interrupted education, limited career options, substance abuse, and loneliness, BPD can indeed be a formidable adversary, especially for those with lesser access to treatment.

Described as a relentless roller coaster ride by sufferers, BPD leads to fluctuating self-perception, changing goals and aspirations, and inconsistent likes and dislikes. This constant sense of uncertainty often leaves those with BPD feeling lost, defensive, and scared.

People with BPD can be extraordinarily sensitive, experiencing life as if they are a raw, exposed nerve. Minor incidents can trigger intense emotional outbursts that can be hard to subside. During such emotional surges, they might say or do things that are hurtful or risky, only to be engulfed by guilt or shame afterward. However, it's important to remember that these actions usually stem from desperation, not a genuine desire to cause harm.

Unfortunately, individuals with BPD can inadvertently wreak havoc in their lives and those around them due to their propensity to misinterpret situations and react impulsively. More often than not, their closest relationships bear the brunt of this disorder, including family, partners, or children.

As with any disorder, it's critical to approach a loved one with BPD with compassion and understanding, recognizing their need for professional help. While your support and care are invaluable, managing BPD isn't a battle to be fought alone. Encourage them to seek professional help and supplement this with your unwavering love and patience.

Emotional Validation and Its Importance

Emotional validation is a powerful tool that can help us build and maintain healthy relationships, but it can be especially important for couples where one partner has borderline personality disorder. It is the act of acknowledging and accepting another person's emotional experience, demonstrating that their feelings are seen, heard, and understood.

When we validate someone's emotions, **we are not saying that we agree with them or that their feelings are justified**. We can validate someone's emotions without agreeing with their thoughts or actions. For example, if your partner is feeling angry, we can validate their anger without agreeing that they are right to be angry. We can simply say, "I understand that you are angry right now. That must be a difficult feeling to have."

Empathy is the ability to understand and share the feelings of another person. It's about putting yourself in their shoes and seeing the world from their perspective. When we empathize with someone, we are able to validate their emotions. This means acknowledging and accepting their feelings as valid, even if we don't agree with them.

Empathy is essential for emotional validation because it helps us to understand why someone is feeling the way they are feeling.

When we understand the root of someone's emotions, we are better able to offer them support and help them to cope.

The Six Levels of Emotional Validation

There are six levels of emotional validation, each of which builds on the previous level:

Level 1: Being Present

The most basic level of emotional validation is simply being present for the person. This means physically being there for them, making eye contact, and showing them that you are listening and paying attention. It also means creating a safe, non-judgmental space where they feel comfortable expressing their emotions.

Level 2: Accurate Reflection

The second level of emotional validation is accurately reflecting the person's emotions. This means summarizing or paraphrasing what they have said, so that they know that you understand their experience. For example, if someone says, "I'm feeling really angry right now," you might say, "It sounds like you're feeling really angry."

Level 3: Mind Reading

The third level of emotional validation is mind reading. This doesn't mean that you have psychic abilities! It means making educated guesses about what the person might be feeling based on the information they have provided. For example, if someone says, "I'm not sure how I feel about this," you might say, "You seem like you might be feeling a little bit confused."

Level 4: Understanding the Person's Behavior in Terms of their History and Biology

The fourth level of emotional validation is understanding the person's behavior in terms of their history and biology. This means recognizing how their past experiences, personal history, or even their biological makeup might be influencing their current feelings. For example, if someone is reacting strongly to a situation because it reminds them of a traumatic event from their past, validating their feelings might involve recognizing this connection.

Level 5: Normalizing or Recognizing Emotional Reactions that Anyone Would Have

The fifth level of emotional validation is normalizing or recognizing emotional reactions that anyone would have. This means recognizing that anyone would likely feel the same way in a similar situation. It can help the person feel less alone or abnormal in their emotional reactions. For example, if someone is anxious about a major life change, you might say, "It's completely normal to feel anxious when you're facing so much uncertainty."

Level 6: Radical Genuineness

The sixth and deepest level of emotional validation is radical genuineness. This occurs when you can relate to the person's feelings on a very personal level, perhaps because you've had a similar experience. It involves expressing this understanding in a genuine, empathetic way. This level of validation can be very powerful, but it must be sincere. It's about saying, "I truly understand how you're feeling because I've been there too."

Emotional validation is a skill that can be practiced and developed over time. It's not about getting it perfect every time, but about striving to create a space where the other person's emotions are seen, heard, and understood.

Shared Coping Strategies

Coping strategies are methods that individuals use to deal with stressful situations, manage their emotions, and reduce anxiety. When one partner in a relationship has BPD, it can be helpful to identify coping strategies that both partners can use. These shared strategies can not only help manage individual stress, but also strengthen the bond between partners and improve communication.

Here are some examples of shared coping strategies:

- **Physical exercise:** Regular physical exercise, such as walking, running, or yoga, can help reduce stress levels and improve mood for both partners. It's an activity that can be done together, fostering a sense of shared accomplishment and mutual support.

- **Mindfulness practices:** Practices like meditation, deep breathing, or progressive muscle relaxation can help both partners become more aware of their emotional state, reduce stress, and stay grounded in the present moment. These practices can be learned together and incorporated into a daily routine.

- **Creative outlets:** Engaging in creative activities together like painting, writing, cooking, or playing music can be therapeutic. It provides an outlet for expressing emotions and can serve as a distraction from stress or anxiety.

- **Listening to music:** Music can be a powerful tool for managing emotions. Creating shared playlists with calming or uplifting songs can be a bonding experience. Listening to this music together during stressful times can help both partners calm down and refocus.

- **Journaling:** While typically an individual activity, journaling can also be used as a shared coping strategy. Partners can agree to journal at the same time about their feelings and thoughts, and if comfortable, they can share and discuss their entries with each other.

- **Therapeutic techniques:** Learning and practicing therapeutic techniques together, such as cognitive restructuring (a cognitive-behavioral technique for identifying and disputing irrational or maladaptive thoughts), can be beneficial. It can help both partners manage their thoughts and emotions more effectively.

- **Nature activities:** Activities like hiking, gardening, or even simply sitting in a park can be calming and grounding. These shared activities can provide a break from daily stressors and offer opportunities for open and relaxed conversations.

These are just a few examples of shared coping strategies that can be helpful for couples where one partner has BPD. It's important to find strategies that work for both partners and that they are both willing to commit to. By working together to manage stress and anxiety, couples can strengthen their bond and build a more resilient relationship.

Regular Check-Ins

Regular check-ins can be a valuable communication tool for partners in a relationship where one person has BPD. BPD is often characterized by intense emotional experiences and fears of abandonment, which can lead to misunderstandings, conflicts, and emotional distress. Regular check-ins offer a structured, safe space to openly discuss feelings, concerns, and issues that arise within the relationship.

Here are some things to keep in mind when having regular check-ins:

- **Set a schedule.** Decide together how often you want to have check-ins. This could be daily, weekly, or bi-weekly, depending on what works best for your relationship.

- **Create a safe space.** These check-ins should be a time when both partners feel safe to express their feelings without fear of judgment or criticism. This might involve setting some ground rules, such as agreeing to listen without interrupting, not using blaming language, and being open to hearing each other's perspectives.

- **Talk about the relationship.** Discuss how you both feel about the relationship. This can include positive aspects, areas that need improvement, and ways to support each other better. It might also be helpful to talk about BPD symptoms and how they're impacting the relationship, as well as discussing strategies for managing these symptoms.

- **Express feelings.** Both partners should feel free to express their feelings about recent events or issues that have come up. The partner with BPD might use this time to talk about their emotional experiences and any challenges they've been facing, while the other partner can share their feelings and any concerns they have.

- **Problem-solve.** If there are specific issues or conflicts that need to be addressed, use this time to problem-solve together. This might involve brainstorming solutions, discussing strategies for managing similar situations in the future, or seeking compromise on contentious issues.

- **Celebrate progress.** Use these check-ins as an opportunity to acknowledge and celebrate progress, no matter how small. This might involve recognizing efforts to use new coping strategies, improvements in communication, or any other positive changes.

By having regular check-ins, partners can ensure that they're on the same page, preemptively address potential issues, and foster a deeper understanding and empathy for each other's experiences. This can be particularly beneficial in the context of BPD, where misunderstandings and emotional intensity can often lead to relationship stress.

Setting and Respecting Boundaries

Setting and respecting boundaries is important in any relationship, but it can be even more important when one partner has borderline personality disorder. BPD can be characterized by intense emotions and fears of abandonment, which can make it difficult to maintain healthy boundaries.

Boundaries are guidelines for how we want to be treated, and they help us distinguish our needs, desires, and limits from those of others. They are essential for maintaining our self-identity, protecting our emotional health, and fostering mutual respect and understanding in our relationships.

Here are some tips for setting and respecting boundaries in a relationship with a person with borderline personality disorder:

- **Identify your personal boundaries.** What are your needs and limits? What makes you feel comfortable or uncomfortable? Take some time to think about these things and what you need in order to feel safe and respected in your relationship.

- **Communicate your boundaries clearly and respectfully.** It's important to be honest and direct with your partner about your boundaries. Explain why these boundaries are important to you and how they help you feel safe and respected.

- **Respect your partner's boundaries.** Just as it's important for you to have your boundaries respected, it's also important to respect your partner's boundaries. This means not crossing their boundaries, even if you don't understand them or agree with them.

- **Navigate boundary violations calmly and assertively.** If your partner does cross your boundary, it's important to address the issue calmly and assertively. Explain why their behavior was unacceptable and how it made you feel.

- **Be flexible and willing to reassess your boundaries.** As your relationship grows and changes, your boundaries may need to change as well. Be open to discussing your boundaries with your partner and making adjustments as needed.

By setting and respecting boundaries, you can help protect your own emotional health, maintain your individuality, and prevent enmeshment in your relationship. This can be especially important in relationships with BPD, as it can provide a sense of stability and predictability, helping to manage some of the challenges associated with the disorder.

Practicing Patience and Consistency

Managing BPD in a relationship can be a long-term process, with ups and downs. It is important for both partners to be patient and consistent with each other.

Patience

BPD can lead to intense emotional reactions, impulsivity, and fear of abandonment. It is important for both partners to understand that managing BPD takes time. The partner without BPD should try to be patient with their loved one, remembering that setbacks do not mean failure. The person with BPD should also be patient with themselves, understanding that progress may be slow and not always steady.

Consistency

In a relationship where one partner has BPD, consistency can create a sense of safety and predictability. This involves consistently implementing coping strategies, maintaining regular communication, and consistently respecting each other's boundaries. Consistent responses to emotional crises or intense situations can also help the person with BPD learn to predict and trust their partner's reactions, which can contribute to a sense of stability.

Positive Reinforcement

Positive reinforcement can be a powerful tool in managing BPD within a relationship. It involves acknowledging and praising each other's efforts, improvements, and successes, no matter how small they might seem.

Recognize Efforts

Both partners should make a conscious effort to recognize and acknowledge each other's attempts to manage the challenges posed by BPD. This could involve noticing when the person with BPD uses a new coping strategy, or when the other partner successfully provides emotional validation.

Celebrate Successes

Celebrate successes, even small ones. Successfully managing a single emotional episode, effectively communicating during a difficult conversation, or respecting a boundary in a challenging situation all warrant recognition. This can help build confidence and motivation to continue making positive changes.

Offer Encouragement

Words of encouragement can go a long way in boosting morale and reinforcing positive behaviors. Genuine, supportive comments can help both partners feel valued and appreciated, fostering a more positive relationship dynamic.

Provide Rewards

Besides verbal reinforcement, consider providing tangible rewards. These don't have to be extravagant or costly; they could be as simple as a favorite meal, a love note, or an evening doing a favorite activity together.

By practicing patience and consistency and employing positive reinforcement, both partners can contribute to a more positive, stable relationship environment, encouraging continued growth and progress in managing BPD.

Managing a relationship with a partner who has BPD can be challenging, but it is possible to do so with empathy, understanding, and support. Let's take a moment to reflect on what we've talked about so far:

Key Points:

- **Emotional validation and empathy are essential in relationships where one partner has BPD.** When you validate your partner's emotions, you are letting them know that you understand and accept their feelings, even if you don't agree with them. This can help to reduce emotional dysregulation and foster a sense of safety and trust in the relationship.

- **There are six levels of emotional validation: being present, accurate reflection, mind reading, understanding the person's behavior in terms of their history and biology, normalizing or recognizing emotional reactions that anyone would have, and radical genuineness.** Each of these levels can be helpful in different ways, so it is important to find what works best for you and your partner.

- **Shared coping strategies can be a great way to manage BPD in a relationship.** These strategies can help you and your partner to deal with difficult emotions, manage stress, and build resilience. Some examples of shared coping strategies include physical exercise, mindfulness practices, creative outlets, listening to music, journaling, learning and practicing therapeutic techniques, and engaging in nature activities.

- **Regular check-ins can be helpful in managing BPD in a relationship.** These check-ins can provide a space for you and your partner to discuss the relationship, express your feelings, problem-solve, and celebrate progress.

- **Setting and respecting boundaries is important in relationships where one partner has BPD.** Boundaries can help to protect your own emotional health and create a sense of safety and predictability in the relationship. It is important to be clear about your boundaries and to respect your partner's boundaries as well.

- **Patience and consistency are essential in managing BPD.** BPD is a complex disorder, and it takes time and effort to manage. It is important to be patient with yourself and your partner, and to be consistent with the strategies that you are using.

- **Positive reinforcement can be a helpful tool in managing BPD.** When you reinforce positive behaviors, you are encouraging your partner to continue those behaviors. This can help to build confidence and motivation, and it can also make the relationship more enjoyable for both of you.

Now that we have a good understanding of how to support a loved one with borderline personality disorder, let's explore the dynamics of manipulation and how partners, family members, and friends can protect themselves from manipulation by people with BPD.

CHAPTER 17: UNDERSTANDING AND DISARMING MANIPULATIVE BEHAVIORS

Have you ever felt manipulated by someone with BPD? If so, how did you deal with it?

Dealing with someone with borderline personality disorder can be challenging. They may try to manipulate you by **making you feel guilty, helpless, or hostile**. This is because people with BPD often have a history of trauma or abuse, and they may recreate these dynamics in their relationships in an attempt to feel safe or in control.

It's important to remember that you are not to blame for the other person's behavior. You cannot control their actions, but you can control how you respond. If you react in anger or frustration, it will only make the situation worse. Instead, try to stay calm and objective.

In this chapter, we will discuss some strategies for understanding and disarming manipulative behaviors. We will also talk about the importance of setting boundaries and taking care of yourself.

Why People with BPD Manipulate

There are a few reasons why people with BPD might manipulate others. One reason is that they may have learned to use manipulation as a way to get their needs met in childhood. If they grew up in a chaotic or abusive household, they may have learned that the only way to get attention or care was to act out or manipulate others.

Another reason why people with BPD might manipulate others is that they have a hard time regulating their emotions. They may feel intense emotions very quickly, and they may not know how to express those emotions in a healthy way. As a result, they may resort to manipulation as a way to get their needs met or to avoid feeling overwhelmed by their emotions.

How to Deal with Manipulative Behavior

If you are dealing with someone with BPD who is using manipulative behavior, it is important to remember a few things:

What Not to Do:

Do not make undue sacrifices. It is important to respect your own needs and not to put yourself in a position where you are sacrificing your own well-being to help someone with BPD. This means not staying up all night talking on the phone with them if you have work the next day, not lending them money you cannot afford, and not rearranging your entire schedule to fit in with their rapidly changing plans. It is important to remember that you cannot help someone if you are not taking care of yourself.

Do not get defensive. It is easy to feel defensive when someone with BPD is being aggressive or hostile, but it is important to avoid reacting in this way. Defensiveness will only escalate the situation. Instead, try to stay calm and objective. If you can, try to understand why the person is feeling the way they are. This will help you to respond in a way that is helpful and supportive.

Do not act hostile. Similarly, it is important to avoid acting hostile towards someone with BPD. This will only make the situation worse. If you are feeling angry or frustrated, try to take a few deep breaths and calm down before you respond. It is also helpful to remember that the person's behavior is not a reflection of you. It is a reflection of their own internal struggles.

Do not feel guilty. It is important to remember that the behavior of someone with BPD is not your fault. You should not feel guilty for their actions. It is important to remember that they are struggling with a mental illness, and that their behavior is not a reflection of your worth as a person.

Do not lecture them. It is unlikely that lecturing someone with BPD will be effective. They may become defensive or argumentative. Instead, try to have a calm and rational conversation with them. If you need to, you can try to educate them about BPD, but do not do this in a way that is condescending or judgmental.

Do not act superior. It is important to remember that everyone is struggling in their own way. Do not act superior to someone with BPD. This will only make them feel worse and make it more difficult to have a productive conversation.

Do not censor issues. If difficult issues arise, it is important to address them in a calm and rational way. Do not try to suppress or avoid these issues. If someone with BPD is struggling with suicidal thoughts or self-harm, it is important to talk to them about it. This does not mean that you have to solve their problems for them, but it does mean that you should be there to listen and offer support.

Do not attempt to deal with suicide attempts on your own. If someone with BPD attempts suicide, it is important to get them help immediately. Do not attempt to deal with this situation on your own. Call 911 or take the person to the nearest emergency room.

What to Do:

Understand and acknowledge their strengths. People with BPD often have a high level of interpersonal skills. They may be very charismatic and charming, and they may be able to connect with people on a deep level. This is because they have learned to adapt to their environment and to the people around them. They may have developed these skills as a way to cope with their BPD symptoms, such as their fear of abandonment.

Acknowledge their strengths and validate their emotions. This will help them feel understood and supported. For example, if someone with BPD tells you that they are feeling scared, you could say something like, "I understand that you're feeling scared. It's normal to feel scared when you're feeling abandoned."

Stay calm. When disagreements arise, it is important to stay calm. People with BPD are often sensitive to criticism, and they may react in an emotional way. If you stay calm, you will be better able to communicate your point of view and help them to see things from your perspective.

For example, if someone with BPD says something that you disagree with, you could say something like, "I can see that you're feeling upset. I'm not trying to criticize you. I just want to understand your point of view."

Be honest. If you make a mistake, admit it. However, do not accept blame for things you did not do. This will only make the situation worse.

For example, if someone with BPD accuses you of something that you didn't do, you could say something like, "I didn't do that. I'm sorry that you feel that way."

Set boundaries. It is important to set clear boundaries with people with BPD. This includes setting limits on acceptable language, aggression, and violence. If a boundary is crossed, disengage and remove yourself from the situation. This will help to convey that inappropriate behavior will not be tolerated.

For example, if someone with BPD starts to use abusive language, you could say something like, "I will not tolerate you speaking to me that way. If you continue, I will leave."

Pay attention to your tone of voice. The tone of your voice can have a big impact on how your message is received. Even if you are trying to defuse a situation, sounding anxious or nervous can undermine your efforts. Practice speaking in a firm, confident, and straightforward manner.

For example, if someone with BPD is getting upset, you could say something like, "I can see that you're getting upset. Let's take a break and come back to this conversation when we've both had a chance to calm down."

Disagree, rather than invalidate. People with BPD may make exaggerated or dramatic statements. Instead of invalidating these statements, find the grain of truth in them and acknowledge that. This way, you are recognizing their feelings without fully accepting the exaggeration.

For example, if someone with BPD says, "You're the worst person in the world," you could say something like, "I know you're feeling angry right now. It's understandable that you would feel that way. But I'm not the worst person in the world. I care about you, and I'm here for you.

Accept moments of helplessness. It is common for people with BPD to make demands that cannot be met. This can lead to feelings of helplessness and guilt for you. It is important to remember that these moments are common and often stem from the person's intense emotional dysregulation and their tendency to place responsibility for their feelings on others.

For example, if someone with BPD asks you to drop everything and come over to their house right away, you might feel helpless if you cannot do so. It is important to remember that you are not responsible for their feelings, and that you cannot always meet their demands. You can try to explain that you are unable to come over right away, but that you will be there as soon as you can.

It is also important to set boundaries with people with BPD. This means letting them know what you are and are not willing to do. For example, you might let them know that you are willing to talk to them on the phone, but that you are not willing to come over to their house if they are feeling angry or upset.

Respond calmly to illogical statements. People with BPD may sometimes express thoughts or emotions that seem illogical, such as claiming a need for harmful substances or behaviors. It is important to respond to these statements in a calm and validating way, even if you do not agree with them. Validation does not mean agreement, but rather acknowledgment of their feelings and experiences.

For example, if someone with BPD tells you that they need to take drugs to feel better, you could say something like, "I understand that you're feeling really down right now. I can see why you might think that drugs would help. But I'm worried about you taking drugs. They can be really dangerous."

It is important to avoid arguing with people with BPD about their illogical statements. This will only make them feel more defensive and less likely to listen to you. Instead, focus on validating their feelings and offering your support.

Find the true meaning beneath hostile comments. Communication with people with BPD can often be layered with complex emotions. A seemingly hostile remark might actually be an expression of fear, insecurity, or frustration. It is important to try and understand these hidden meanings and respond to them appropriately. This approach requires empathetic listening and patience, but it can lead to more constructive interactions.

For example, if someone with BPD says something like, "You're always trying to control me," you could try to understand what they are really feeling. Are they feeling insecure? Are they feeling like you are not listening to them? Once you understand what they are really feeling, you can respond in a way that addresses their underlying emotions.

Be conscious of attempts at creating division. People with BPD may sometimes engage in splitting, a defensive mechanism where others are viewed as all good or all bad. This can cause conflicts within families or treatment teams as they may provide different feedback or perspectives to different people. Being aware of this possibility can help to prevent unnecessary conflict and maintain a united front that is in the best interest of the person with BPD.

For example, if someone with BPD tells you that their therapist is "stupid" and "doesn't understand them," you could try to understand why they are saying this. Are they feeling like their therapist is not listening to them? Are they feeling like their therapist is not on their side? Once you understand why they are saying this, you can try to talk to them about it in a way that is helpful and supportive.

Own up to your mistakes. Interactions with people with BPD can be intense and challenging. There may be times when you react or behave in ways that you did not intend to. It is important to acknowledge and apologize for any harm you have caused. Owning up to your mistakes builds trust and models accountability, two key components in building a positive relationship with a person suffering from BPD.

At the same time, remember to express how you felt at that moment, thus emphasizing the reciprocal nature of emotions in any interaction.

For example, if you say something hurtful to someone with BPD, you could say something like, "I'm so sorry that I said that. I didn't mean to hurt you. I was feeling really angry at the time, and I took it out on you. That was wrong of me, and I'm really sorry."

It is important to be sincere when you apologize to someone with BPD. They need to know that you are truly sorry for what you did, and that you are committed to doing better in the future.

Managing BPD in relationships can be challenging, especially when manipulation comes into play. In this chapter, we will explore the reasons behind manipulative behaviors in individuals with BPD and provide practical strategies for understanding, disarming these behaviors, and taking care of oneself.

Key Points:

Why do people with BPD manipulate? Individuals with BPD may resort to manipulation for a variety of reasons. Some common reasons include:

- **History of chaos or abuse:** People with BPD may have learned manipulation as a survival strategy in childhood. If they grew up in chaotic or abusive environments, they may have learned that manipulation is the only way to get their needs met or to avoid feeling overwhelmed by intense emotions.

- **Difficulty regulating emotions:** People with BPD often have difficulty regulating their emotions. This can lead them to manipulate as a way to meet their needs or avoid feeling overwhelmed by intense emotions.

How to deal with manipulative behavior: There are a number of things you can do to deal with manipulative behavior in individuals with BPD. These include:

- **Do not make undue sacrifices:** It is important to set boundaries and not make undue sacrifices for someone who is manipulating you. This will only reinforce their manipulative behavior.

- **Avoid defensiveness, hostility, and guilt:** It is also important to avoid becoming defensive, hostile, or guilt-ridden when someone with BPD is manipulating you. This will only escalate the situation.

- **Refrain from lecturing or acting superior:** It is important to remember that people with BPD often have difficulty regulating their emotions. Lecturing or acting superior will only make them feel worse and make the situation worse.

Positive strategies: There are also a number of positive strategies you can adopt when dealing with manipulative behavior. These include:

- **Acknowledge their strengths:** It is important to acknowledge the strengths of people with BPD. This will help them feel valued and respected, and it may make them less likely to resort to manipulation.

- **Stay calm during disagreements:** It is also important to stay calm during disagreements with people with BPD. This will help to de-escalate the situation and prevent it from getting worse.

- **Be honest:** It is important to be honest with people with BPD, even if it is difficult. Honesty will help to build trust and prevent them from feeling like they have to manipulate you to get their needs met.

- **Set clear boundaries:** It is important to set clear boundaries with people with BPD. This will help them understand what is and is not acceptable behavior.

- **Pay attention to your tone of voice:** It is also important to pay attention to your tone of voice when interacting with people with BPD. A harsh or condescending tone will only make them feel worse and make the situation worse.

- **Understand the true meaning beneath hostile comments:** Sometimes, people with BPD will make hostile comments that do not actually reflect their true feelings. It is important to try to understand the true meaning behind these comments before reacting.

- **Be conscious of attempts at creating division:** People with BPD may sometimes try to create division between you and other people in your life. It is important to be aware of these attempts and to not let them get to you.

- **Taking care of oneself:** It is also important to take care of oneself when dealing with manipulative behavior. This includes taking breaks, getting support from others, and practicing self-care.

Lastly, we emphasized the importance of accepting moments of helplessness and owning up to one's mistakes. In interactions with individuals with BPD, it's crucial to understand their intense emotional dysregulation and their tendency to place responsibility for their feelings on others. Acknowledging any harm caused and apologizing sincerely can help build trust and model accountability.

In some cases, it may not be possible to continue a relationship with someone with borderline personality disorder. **If you are** in serious difficulty dating a loved one with BPD, it is important to prioritize your safety and well-being. The next chapter is designed to help you make the best decision for yourself.

CHAPTER 18: BREAKING UP WITH A LOVED ONE WITH BORDERLINE PERSONALITY DISORDER

Have you ever wondered what it's like to break up with someone who is terrified of being abandoned?

Breaking up with someone who has BPD can be a difficult and daunting task. People with BPD often have a heightened sensitivity to rejection, and they may react in unpredictable and potentially harmful ways. This can make it feel like you are walking on eggshells, and it can be hard to know how to end the relationship in a way that is both respectful and safe.

Before we get into the heart of this important and controversial chapter, I want to address a sensitive issue: when is it appropriate to break up with someone with BPD? What are the conditions under which it is better to cut ties instead of continuing the relationship?

Ending a relationship is a personal decision, and there is no one-size-fits-all answer. However, if the relationship is causing you severe emotional, physical, or psychological harm, it may be time to consider ending it.

Here are some signs that it might be appropriate to end the relationship:

- **Abuse:** If your partner is abusive, whether physically, emotionally, or verbally, it is never acceptable. If they show no signs of willingness to seek help or change, it may be time to end the relationship.

- **Consistent unhappiness:** If you are consistently unhappy in the relationship, feel drained, or are experiencing severe stress, it might be time to consider breaking up. While all relationships have their ups and downs, the overall trend should be positive.

- **Lack of respect:** Mutual respect is essential in any relationship. If your partner consistently disrespects you or disregards your feelings, it could be a sign that the relationship isn't healthy.

- **Lack of growth:** If your partner is unwilling to seek help for their BPD, refuses to acknowledge their disorder, or doesn't show signs of growth or change, it might be time to leave. This is especially true if their behavior is harmful to you or others.

- **Effects on personal life:** If the relationship is severely affecting your ability to lead a healthy life - including work, social activities, and self-care - it might be an indication that the relationship is unhealthy.

If you are considering ending the relationship, it is important to do so in a safe and supportive environment. If you are concerned about potential escalation or harmful reactions, it may be helpful to plan your exit strategy with a mental health professional.

Keep in mind, it is important to prioritize your own mental health and well-being. It is okay to end a relationship if it is causing harm.

Imagine being in a relationship with someone who is constantly afraid of being abandoned. They may become clingy and possessive, and they may make threats of self-harm or suicide if you try to leave them. This can be a very emotionally draining and stressful experience.

If you are considering breaking up with someone with BPD, it is important to be aware of the potential risks involved. They may react in a way that is harmful to themselves or to you. It is important to take steps to protect yourself and to ensure that they are safe.

Coping with the Emotional Aftermath of Breaking Up with a Partner with BPD

Allow yourself to end the relationship

Breaking up with someone with BPD can be a difficult decision. You may feel guilty about leaving them, especially if they are struggling with mental health challenges. However, it is important to remember that you are not responsible for their happiness or well-being. If the relationship is making you unhappy, you have the right to end it. **There are many stories of people who have stayed in relationships with people with BPD out of guilt or fear**. They may worry that if they leave, their partner will hurt themselves or even die. However, it is important to remember that you cannot control your partner's actions. If they are going to hurt themselves, they will do it whether you are in the relationship or not. **The most important thing is to take care of yourself**. If the relationship is making you unhappy, it is not worth it to stay in it. You deserve to be happy, and you deserve to be in a relationship that is healthy and supportive.

Be kind and compassionate

Be clear and direct. This means telling your partner that you are breaking up with them, and explaining why. It is important to be honest and upfront, but it is also important to be kind and compassionate. **Avoid going into a lot of detail.** This could be hurtful and make your partner feel worse. If they ask why you are breaking up with them, you can give them a general explanation, but you do not need to go into every detail. **Remember that your partner is likely feeling a lot of pain.** They may be angry, upset, or even scared. Be patient and understanding. Allow them to express their feelings, and listen without judgment.

Allow yourself to mourn the loss

It is normal to feel a sense of loss, emptiness, and grief. This is because you have lost someone who was important to you, even if the relationship was not good for you.

Allow yourself to feel these emotions. Do not try to suppress them or bottle them up. Crying, feeling sad, and missing your partner are all normal and healthy ways to cope with the loss of a relationship. **Give yourself time to grieve.** There is no set amount of time that it takes to grieve a breakup. Everyone is different. Be patient with yourself and allow yourself to heal at your own pace.

Do not judge yourself for your feelings

It is easy to think that if you are feeling sad or angry, you must have made the wrong decision. However, this is not true. It is perfectly normal to feel a range of emotions after a breakup. Remember that you are not alone. Many people have felt the same way after a breakup. There is nothing wrong with you. Be kind to yourself. Give yourself the same compassion and understanding that you would give to a friend who was going through a breakup.

Remind yourself that you made the best decision for yourself

It is important to remember that you made the decision to end the relationship for a reason. There were things about the relationship that were not working for you, and you decided that it was time to move on. Remind yourself of these reasons. Write them down, or talk to a friend or therapist about them. This will help you to stay strong in your decision. Be patient with yourself. It takes time to heal from a breakup. Be patient with yourself and allow yourself to move on at your own pace.

Setting boundaries with an ex-partner with BPD

It is common for people with BPD to continue to contact their ex-partners after the relationship has ended. This is because they have a difficult time accepting rejection and a fear of being alone. It can be challenging to deal with this, but the best thing to do is not engage with them. Doing so will only prolong the pain for both of you.

Your ex-partner may try to get your attention by alternating between accusations, hurtful comments, and expressions of love. Remember that people with BPD often see things in black and white, and they will do whatever they can to regain control and win you back.

It is understandable to feel guilty and fearful when you do not respond to your ex-partner's attempts to contact you. You may worry that they will harm themselves or even attempt suicide. However, you cannot be held responsible for their behavior forever. You need to start putting yourself first.

If you are concerned that your ex-partner may engage in self-harm or suicide, talk to their family members or therapist. You can also remove yourself from the situation as soon as possible.

It is important to remember that you are not responsible for your ex-partner's well-being. You have the right to set boundaries and protect yourself. If they are not willing to respect your boundaries, you need to take steps to distance yourself from them.

Reclaim your belongings with empathy and care.

The end of a relationship can be difficult for anyone, but it can be especially challenging for people with BPD. They may have a hard time accepting the breakup and may try to hang on to your belongings as a way to keep a piece of you. This is not because they are trying to be malicious, but because they are struggling to cope with the loss.

If you are considering leaving a relationship with someone who has BPD, it is a good idea to remove any belongings that you have from their home beforehand. This will help to avoid any potential conflicts or arguments that could arise when you try to reclaim your belongings later. It will also reduce the risk of your belongings being damaged or destroyed.

If you do need to reclaim your belongings from your ex-partner's home, it is important to do so in a way that is empathetic and respectful. Remember that they are likely still struggling with the breakup, and they may not be thinking clearly. Be patient and understanding, and try to avoid triggering any of their emotional triggers.

If you are able to reclaim your belongings in a calm and respectful way, it will help to facilitate a smoother and more amicable breakup. This will be better for both of you in the long run.

Taking care of yourself after a breakup with someone who has BPD

Being in a relationship with someone who has BPD can be emotionally draining, and the constant emotional stress can take a toll on your physical and mental health. It is important to take care of yourself after a breakup, especially if you have been in a relationship with someone who has BPD.

Allow yourself time to grieve, and feel your emotions, both the good and the bad. Do not try to suppress your feelings or bottle them up. Spend time with loved ones who love and support you. Talk to them about what you are going through, and let them know how they can help. Engage in self-care activities that make you feel good, such as yoga, meditation, or spending time in nature. Take care of your physical health by eating healthy foods, getting enough sleep, and exercising regularly.

If you are struggling to cope with the breakup, talking to a therapist or counselor can be helpful. They can provide you with support and guidance as you heal. Remember, you are not alone. Many people have been in relationships with people who have BPD, and they have come out the other side. With time and care, you can heal and move on with your life.

Reflecting on your attachment style after a relationship with someone who has BPD

Now that you have stepped away from a damaging relationship with someone who has BPD, it may be a good time to examine your own attachment issues.

People with BPD often need conflict in their relationships to feel normal and to stave off feelings of emptiness. However, it is also worth asking yourself what drew you to your BPD partner in the first place. Was it their charisma and energy? Or are you yourself carrying attachment issues that led you to seek out a potentially damaging relationship?

People with BPD generally have a strong desire for both physical and emotional intimacy. This can lead them to insecure attachment styles, which can in turn lead to damaging relationships. When people with BPD find themselves in romantic relationships, they often experience chronic stress, abuse at the hands of their partners, and unwanted pregnancies.

It is important to ask yourself whether your relationship with a BPD sufferer was a damaging one for both of you. If so, what role did you play in creating this dynamic?

We learn who to love and how to love from our parents and upbringing. If you grew up with parents who were absent or abusive in any way, these issues may have manifested themselves as an insecure attachment style, leading you to seek out relationships with people who will have a negative effect on you.

In all likelihood, both you and your ex-partner have suffered trauma in your childhood, leading you both to form your relationship. For example, if you were neglected by your parents as a child, you may have learned that the only way to gain attention and praise was to behave in a perfect manner and suppress any negative emotions. This can lead to a people-pleasing personality, which can be attractive to a BPD sufferer.

People with BPD often represent the shadow side of people-pleasers. This is the part of our being that we suppress and prevent from seeing the light of day. It includes our negative emotions such as anger, fear, and jealousy. A person with BPD has no difficulty expressing these emotions, and by pairing yourself with them, you are allowing yourself to become "whole."

Alternatively, you may have grown up in a household of chaos and conflict. If this is the case, you may be recreating the tumultuous environment which feels most natural to you by seeking out a relationship with a BPD sufferer.

Working with a counselor or therapist can help you identify and remove your own attachment issues. By recognizing exactly what drew you towards your ex-partner in the first place, you can address these issues and save yourself the pain of repeating the pattern in future relationships.

We have now completed this complex and challenging chapter. Let's take a moment to reflect on the most important points we have made:

Breaking up with someone who has BPD can be a complex and challenging experience. People with BPD often have a heightened fear of abandonment, which can make the breakup process even more difficult. It is important to remember that you are not responsible for your ex-partner's happiness or well-being, and that you have the right to end the relationship if it is not healthy for you.

Key Points:

- **Breaking up with someone who has BPD can be emotionally challenging.** Be prepared for your ex-partner to experience a range of emotions, including anger, sadness, and fear.

- **It is important to be kind, compassionate, clear, and direct when breaking up.** Avoid unnecessary details that could escalate the situation.

- **It is normal to grieve after a breakup.** Allow yourself to feel the range of emotions without judgment.

- **After the breakup, it is essential to set clear boundaries with your ex-partner.** Do not engage in their attempts to continue contact if it affects your well-being.

- **Reclaim your belongings from your ex-partner in a respectful and empathetic manner.** Avoid possible triggers.

- **Prioritize self-care after the breakup.** Engage in self-care activities, surround yourself with loved ones, and consider therapy if needed.

- **Reflecting on your attachment style post-breakup can offer insight into potential patterns and provide a path for future healthier relationships.**

CONCLUSION

I want to thank you for making it this far in your reading journey. It takes courage to delve into a topic as complex as Borderline Personality Disorder, and I commend your dedication.

Throughout this book, we've explored the many facets of BPD, from its biological underpinnings to the environmental factors that contribute to its development. We've learned that BPD is a legitimate and complex condition with roots in both our biology and our experiences. We've also examined different therapeutic approaches for managing BPD, such as Cognitive Behavioral Therapy and Dialectical Behavioral Therapy. These therapies are collaborative, goal-oriented, and tailored to the individual's needs, offering hope for effective management of the condition.

As we conclude, it's important to remember that the knowledge and strategies presented in this book are not a one-time read. The real value lies in revisiting these pages, reflecting on the insights, and implementing the advice in real-world scenarios. Whether you're someone living with BPD or a loved one offering support, the tools and techniques outlined in this book can serve as a roadmap to a more fulfilling, rewarding life despite the challenges of BPD.

Be kind to yourself

BPD can make you feel like you're not good enough, but that's not true. You are worthy of love and respect, just the way you are. Treat yourself with the same kindness and compassion that you would treat a friend.

Be patient with yourself

You are not alone in this. Many people with BPD struggle with patience. It is important to remember that you are learning a new way to manage your emotions and that it takes time. Be kind to yourself and give yourself the space to make mistakes.

Build a support network

Having people who understand what you're going through can make a big difference. Talk to your friends and family about your diagnosis, and join a support group for people with BPD.

There are also online forums where you can connect with other people with BPD.

Stay informed about BPD

The more you know about it, the better equipped you are to manage it. There are many resources available online and in libraries. Read books, articles, and websites about BPD. Talk to your therapist about your diagnosis and learn as much as you can.

Don't give up

BPD is a challenging condition, but it's not impossible to manage. With patience, self-care, and professional help, you can live a full and meaningful life. Don't give up on yourself. You are capable of achieving great things.

Remember, the path to understanding and managing BPD is not a sprint, but a marathon. It requires patience, persistence, and compassion. But with the right help and support, as this book has hopefully shown, it is entirely possible to navigate this journey successfully.

Thank you once again for your time and dedication. I wish you strength, resilience, and hope on your continued journey with BPD.

www.ingramcontent.com/pod-product-compliance
Lightning Source LLC
Chambersburg PA
CBHW051823150726
47998CB00001B/263